Fave Art 4
Pinoy Art Collection
Self-publisher - Tatay Jobo Elizes
2012

I want to share my favorite art collection via this pictorial book, as if you are looking at a gallery. Please make this a coffee table book and let your friends and visitors enjoy by gifting them this book. You may cut out the images and frame them yourself. You may contact me to order from the artist for original paintings or commissioned art of your own choice.

Captions Guide - Each page description is listed here.

Page 2, Noelle Bowen, Brunette Barbie with Little Boy + + + **Page 3, Noelle Bowen,** Sports Barbie with Ball + + + **Page 4, Noelle Bowen,** Bikini Girl Plus Baby + + + **Page 5, Noelle Bowen,** Lady with Sword + + +**Page 6, Noelle Bowen,** Nude Ladies, ala Picasso + + + **Page 7, Noelle Bowen,** Relaxing Barbie lady + + + **Page 8, Tatay Jobo,** Noelle Bowen Portrait, Enhanced Drawing + + + **Page 9, Nolle Bowen,** Self-Portrait, ala Picasso + + + **Page 10, Noelle Bowen,** Night city skyline + + + **Page 11, Noelle Bowen,** Abstract Painting + (Note: Noelle-Mari Elizes Bowen is my grand-daughter, age 23, who finished Fine Arts at Brooklyn College in New York)

Page 12, Mar-Vic Cagurangan, Daze + + + **Page 13, Mar-Vic Cagurangan,** Deconstruction + + + **Page 14, Mar-Vic Cagurangan,** Enigma + + + **Page 15, Mar-Vic Cagurangan,** Weird + (Note: Mar-Vic Caguranagan is my friend, writer and journalist, based in Guam)

Page 16, Nanet Yatco, Madonna & Child + + + **Page 17, Nanet Yatco,** Madonna + + +**Page 18, Nanet Yatco,** Sonya Garden + + + **Page 19, Nanet Yatco,** Flowery Design + + +**Page 20, Nanet Yatco,** Nude Study + + (Note: The artist name is Nannette Rose Yatco, Dentist, Poet, and Painter, from Daet & Manila, who is my close friend. I asked her to use Nanet, as it rhymes with Monet and Manet)

Page 21, Tatay Jobo, Fort Santiago House, Enhanced Pic + + +**Page 22, Tatay Jobo,** Psychedelic Carabao, Enhanced Pic + + + **Page 23, Tatay Jobo,** Fruit Stand, Enhanced Pic + + + **Page 24, Tatay Jobo,** Nipa Hut (Bahay Kubo), Enhaned Pic + + + **Page 25, Tatay Jobo,** Parrots, Enhanced Pic + + +**Page 26, Tatay Jobo,** Tinkling Dancers, Enhanced Pic + + +**Page 27, Tatay Jobo,** Pool Fishes, Enhanced Pic + + +**Page 28, Tatay Jobo,** Love Birds, Enhanced Pic + (Note: This is my first attempt at creating art, mostly by computer-generated art work and enhancing pictures using available software)

Page 29, Loleng Liwanag, Jar and Fruits + + + **Page 30, Loleng Liwanag,** Modern Painting + + + **Page 31, Loleng Liwanag,** Bananas + Other Fruits, Still + + + **Page 32, Loleng Liwanag,** Dramatic Pose + (Note: Ate Loleng is Dolores Cabuso Liwanag, my first cousin, who recently died. She taught English and Literature at UP for many years)

Page 33, Hermes Alegre, Cute Face + + + **Page 34, Hermes Alegre,** Typical Filipina + + + **Page 35, Hermes Alegre,** School Girl Look + + + **Page 36, Hermes Alegre,** Rural Modonna & Child + + + **Page 37, Hermes Alegre,** Chinita Girl + + + **Page 38, Hermes Alegre,** Three Lovely Faces + + + (Note: Hermes Alegre is already a famous Artist in Philippines and abroad. He is from Daet, my hometown)

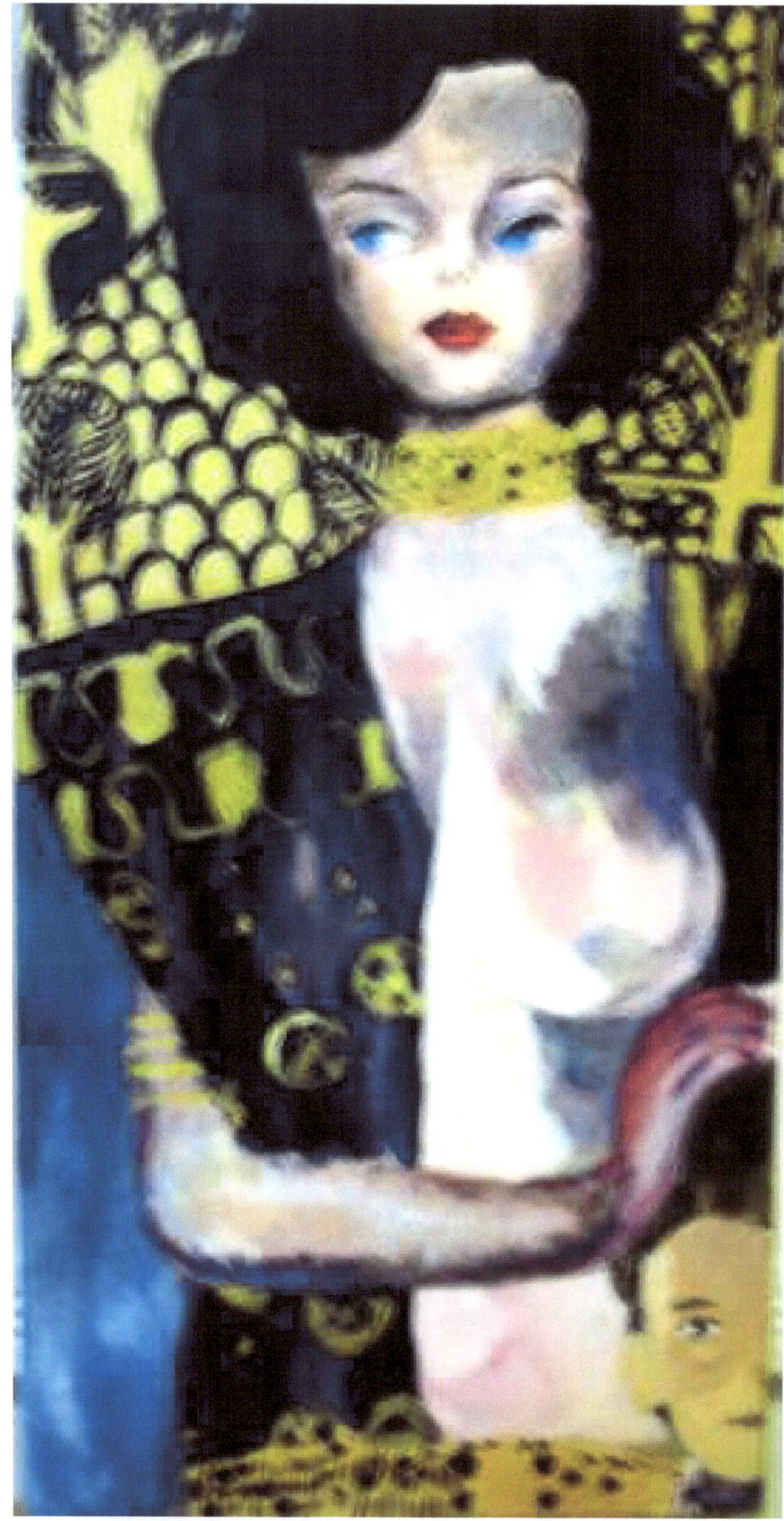

Noelle Bowen, Brunette Barbie with Little Boy

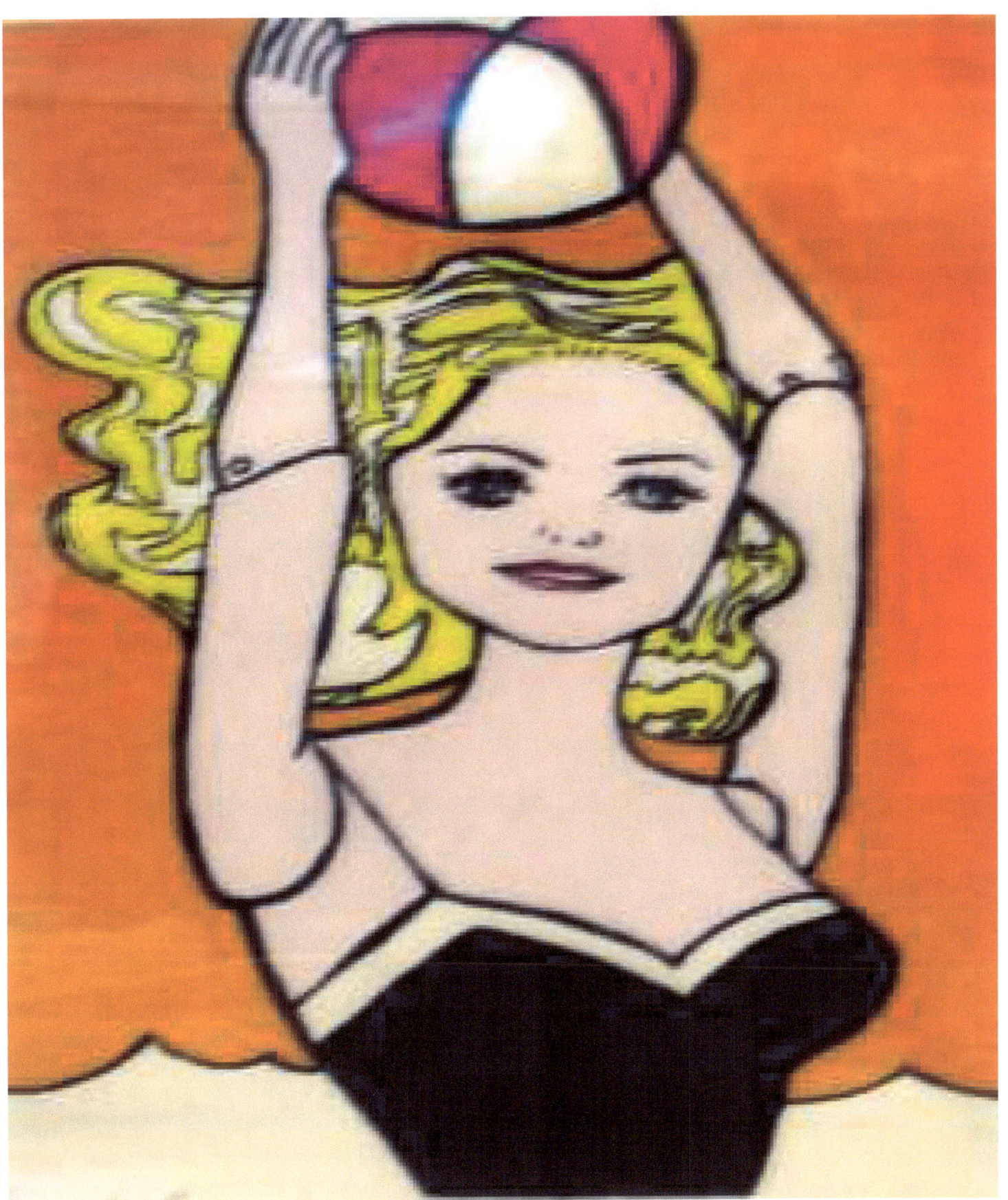

Noelle Bowen, Sports Barbie with Ball

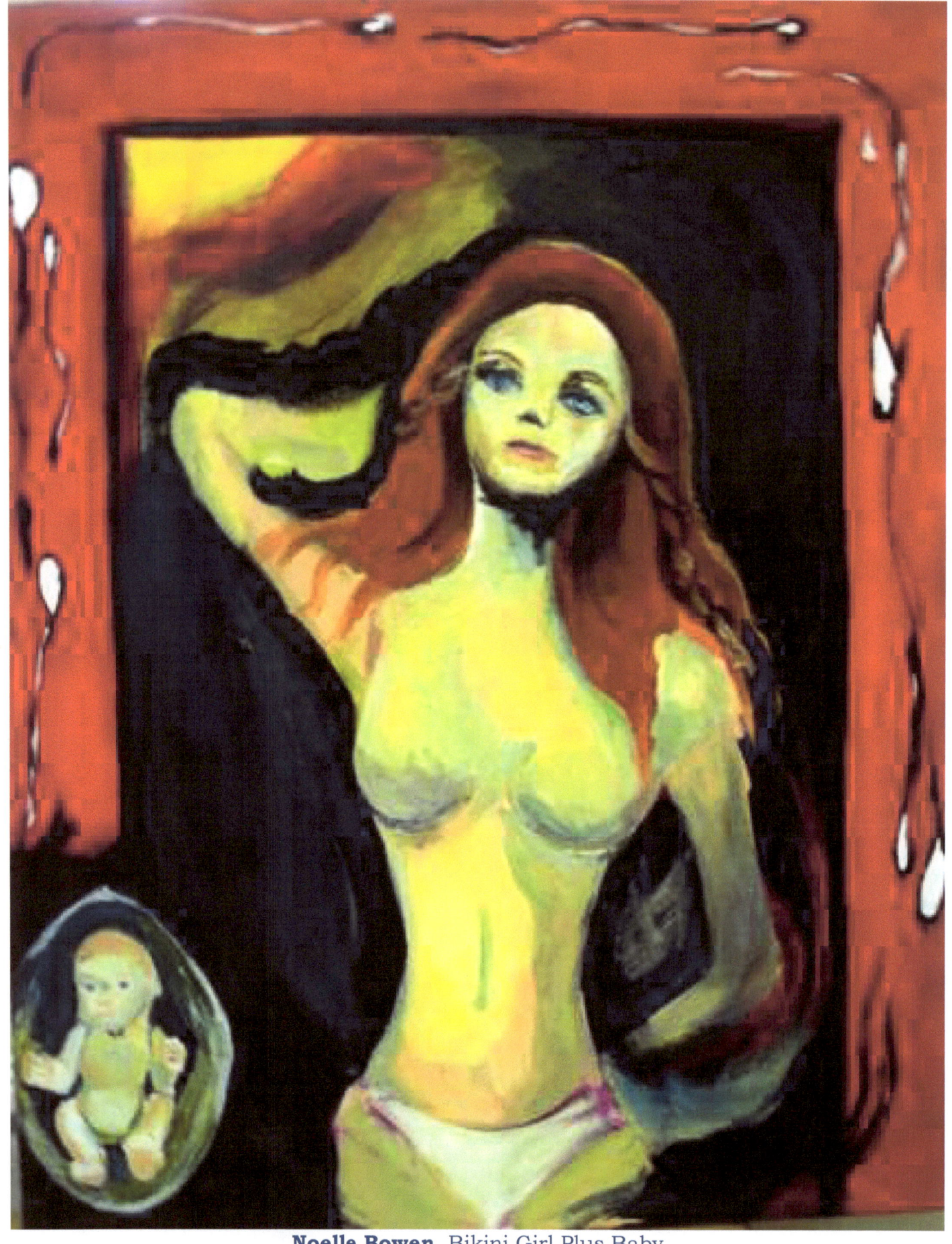

Noelle Bowen, Bikini Girl Plus Baby

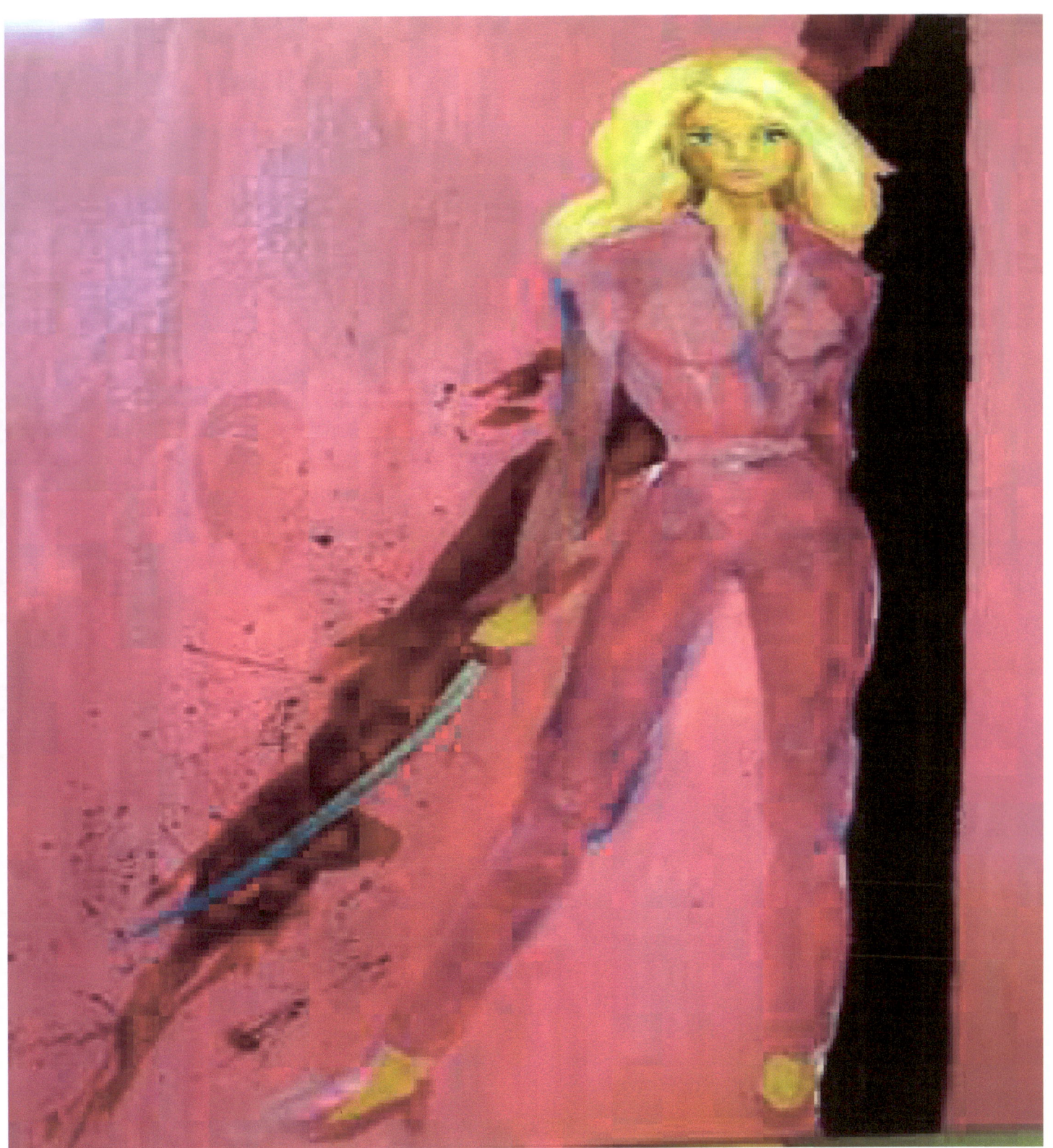

Noelle Bowen, Lady with Sword

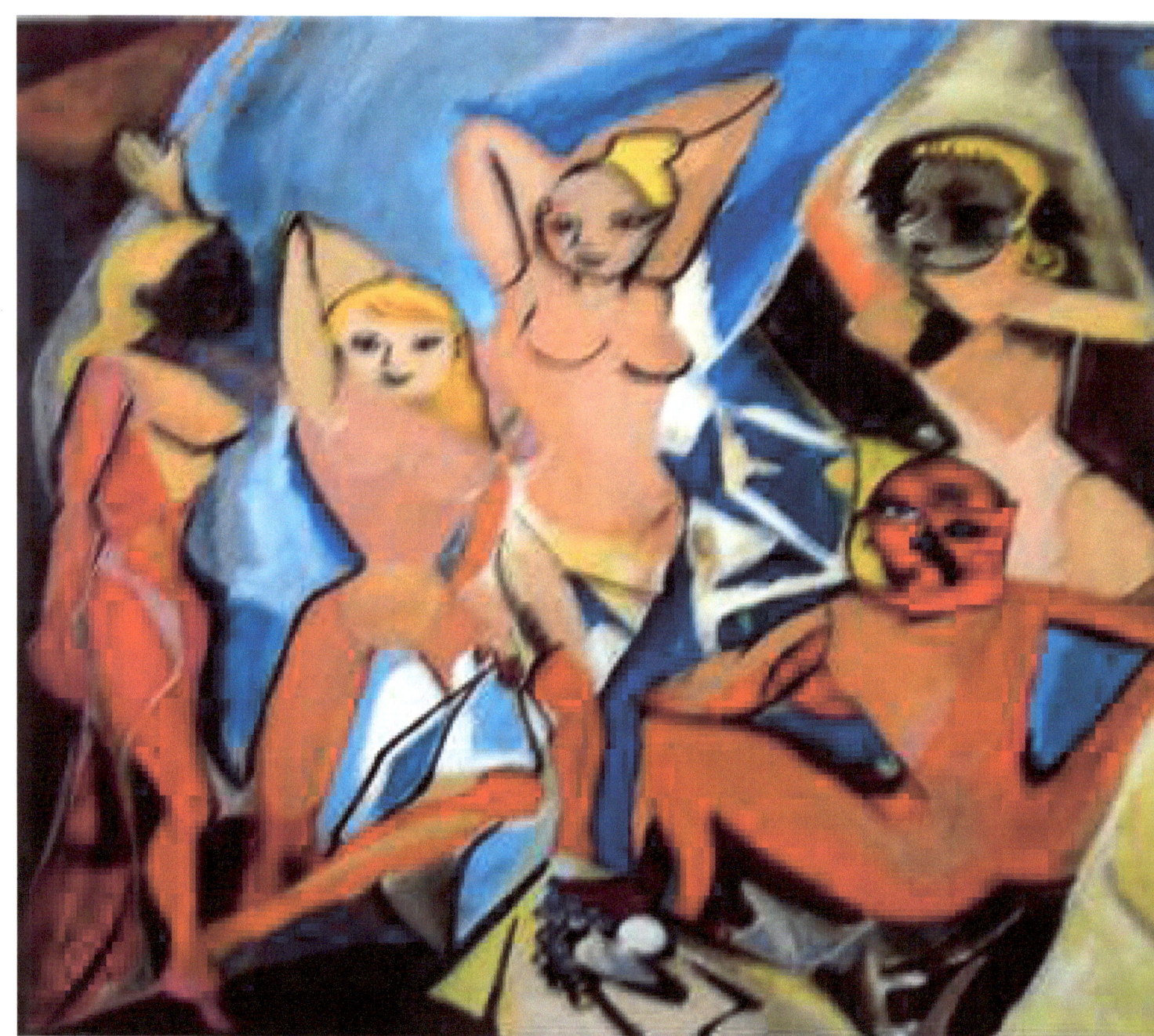

Noelle Bowen, Nude Ladies, ala Picasso

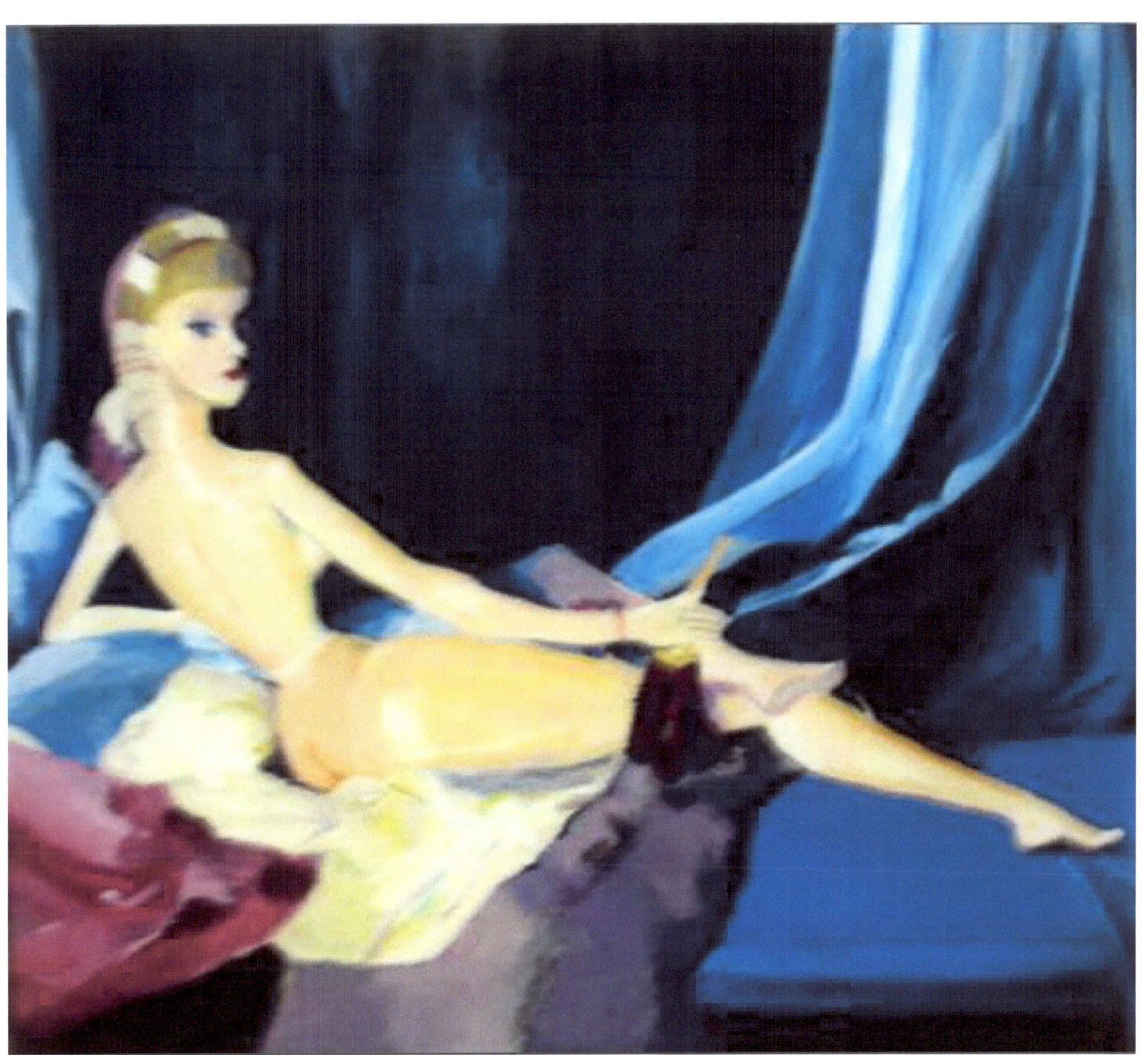

Noelle Bowen, Relaxing Barbie lady

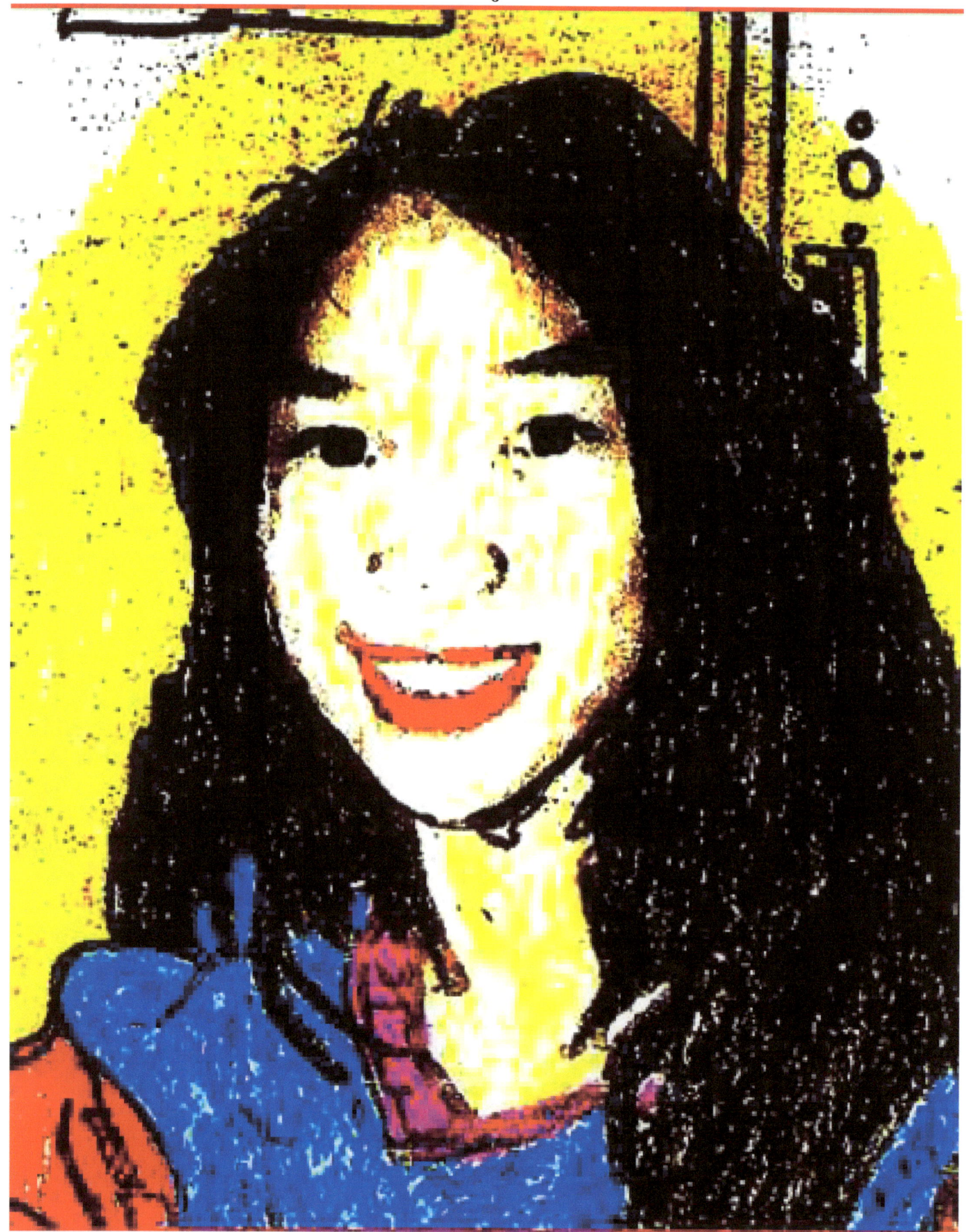

Tatay Jobo, Noelle Bowen Portrait, Enhanced Drawing

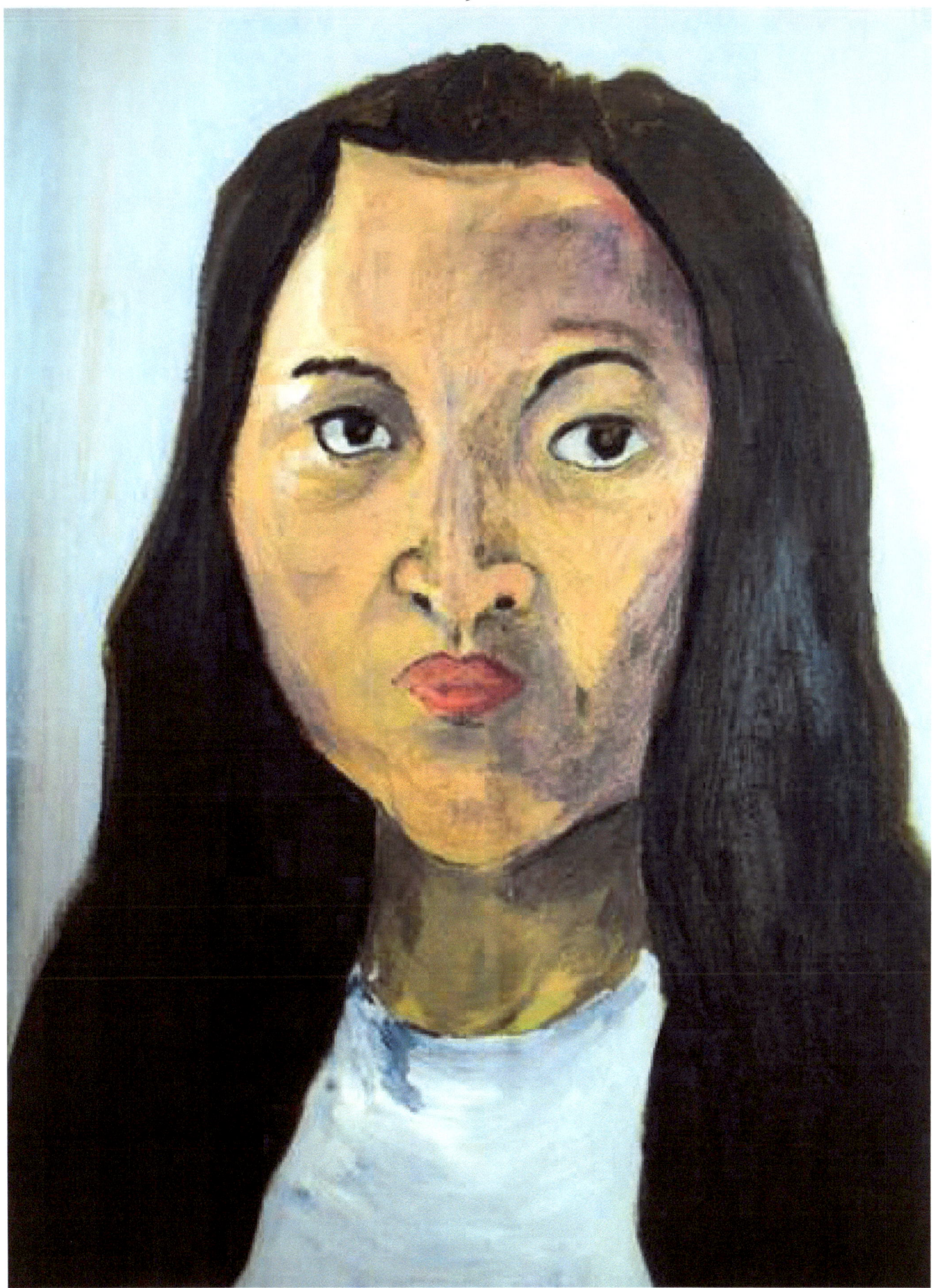

Noelle Bowen, Self-Portrait, ala Picasso

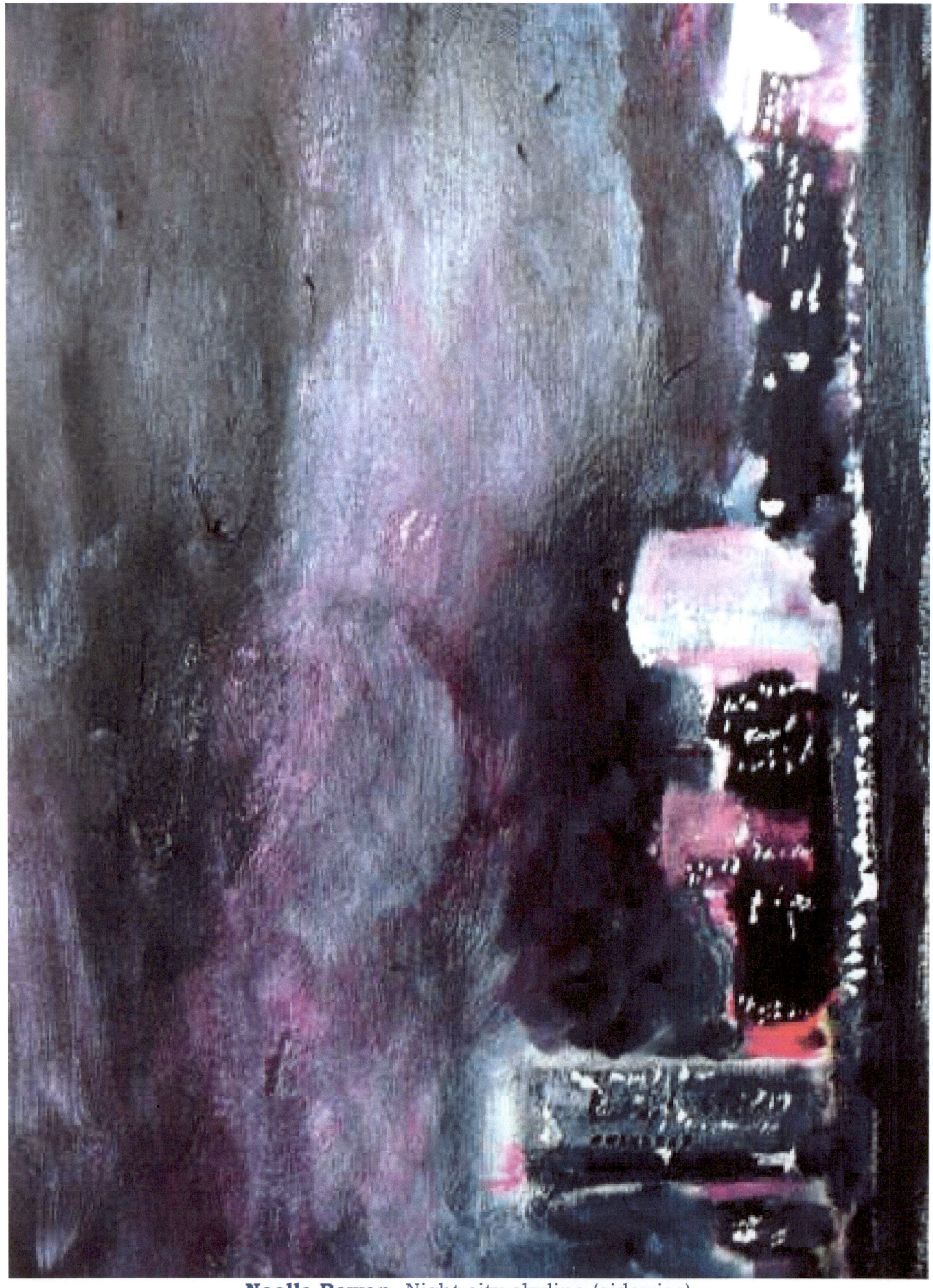

Noelle Bowen, Night city skyline (sidewise)

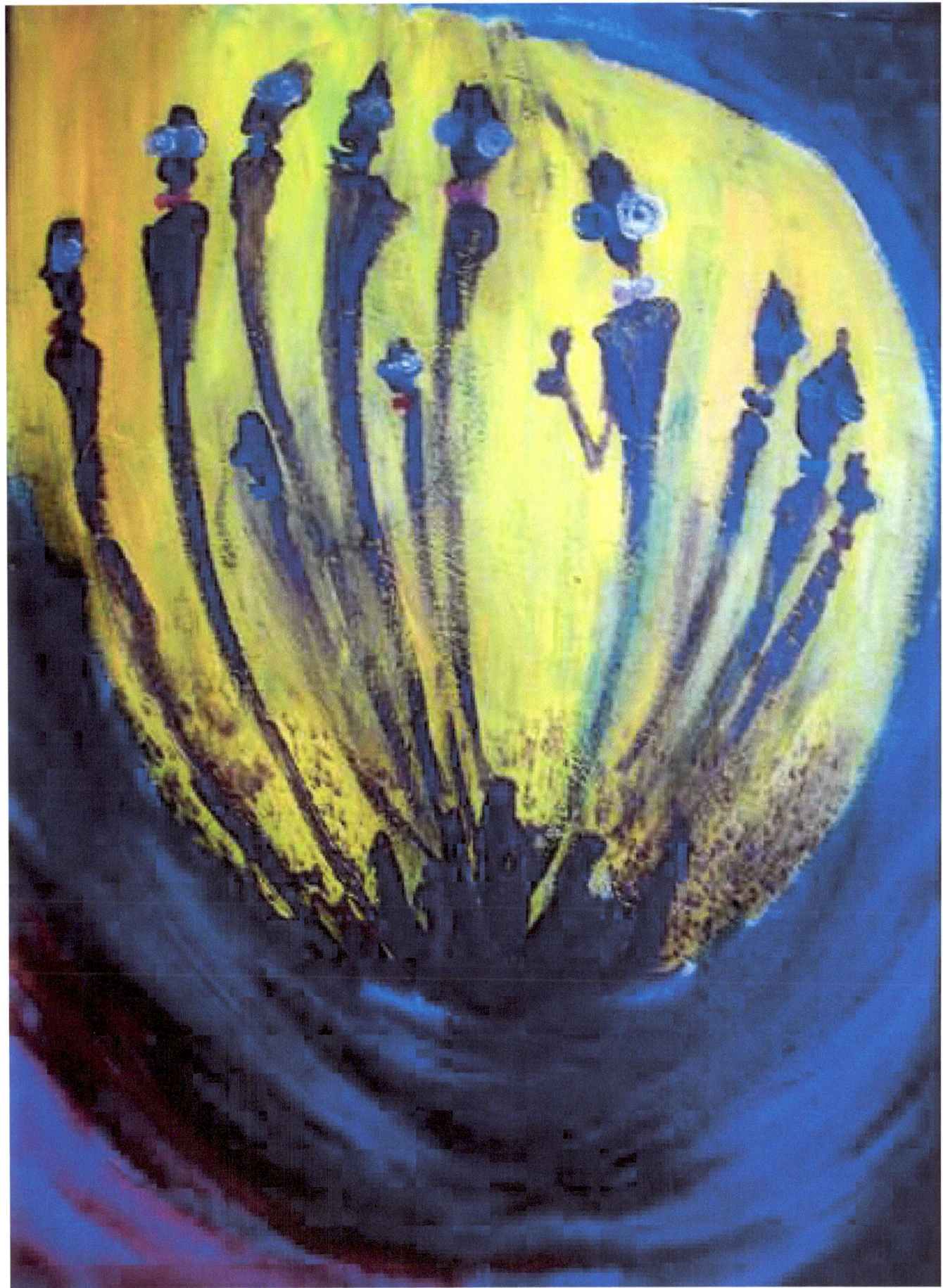

Noelle Bowen, Abstract Painting

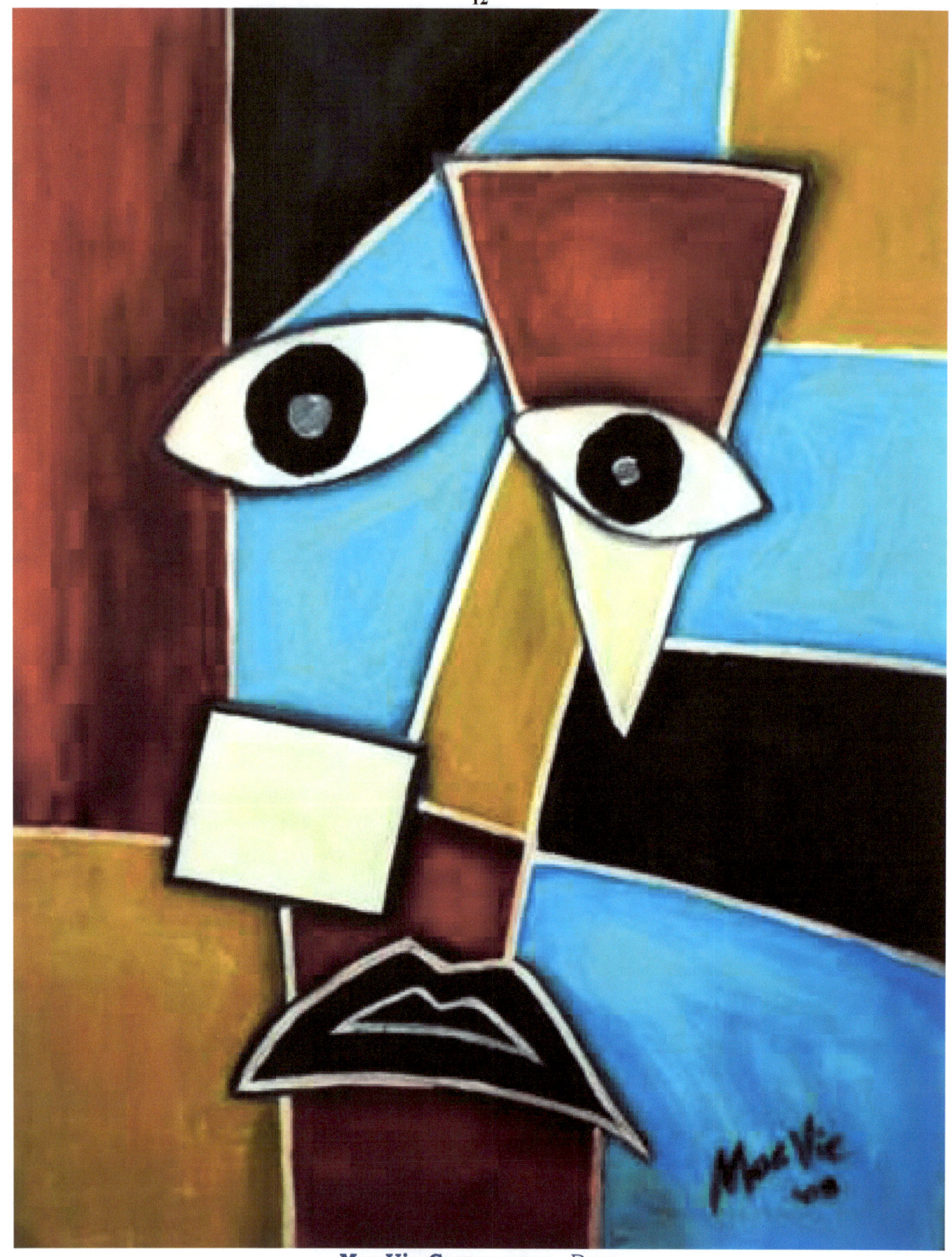

Mar-Vic Cagurangan, Daze

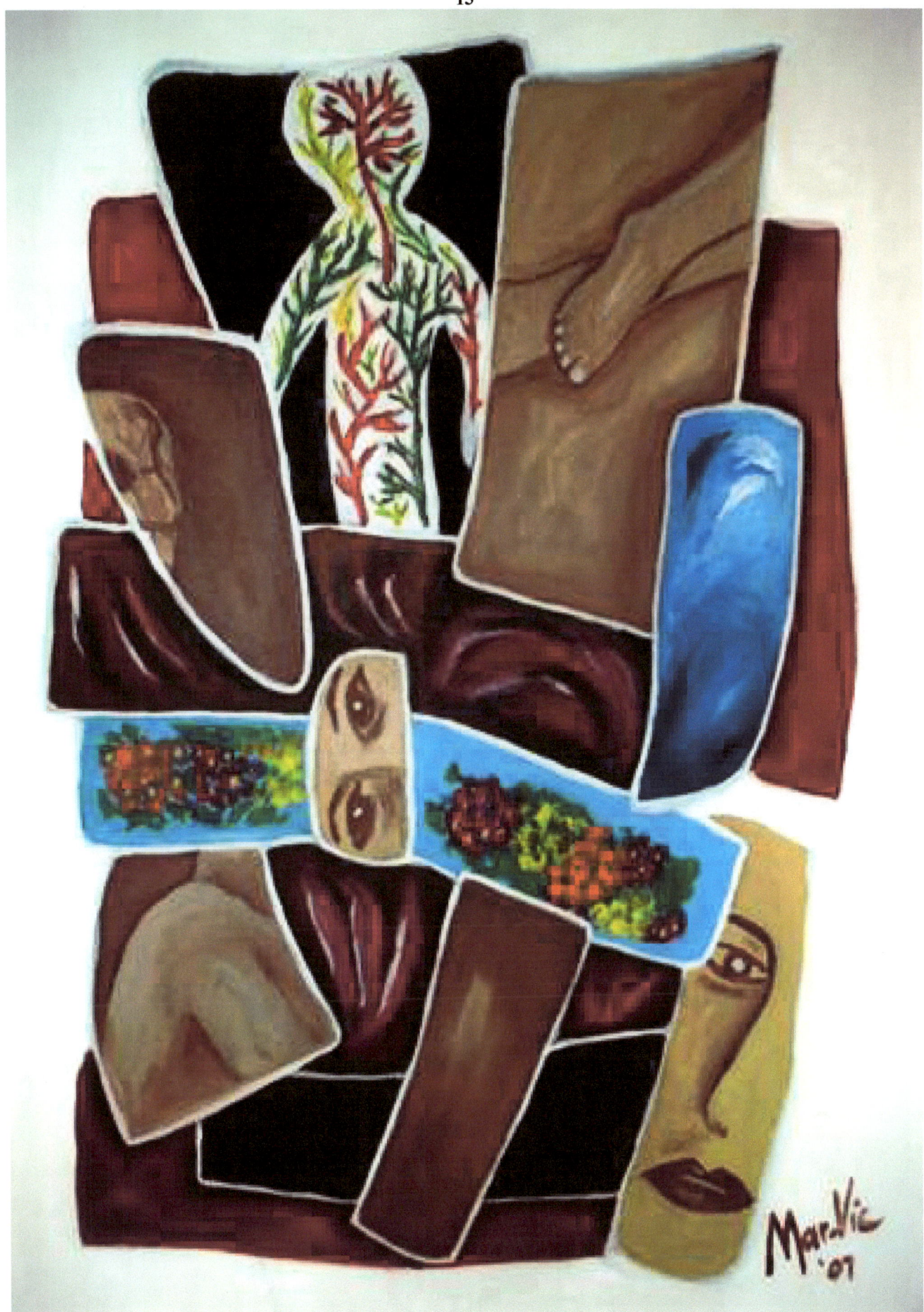

Mar-Vic Cagurangan, Deconstruction

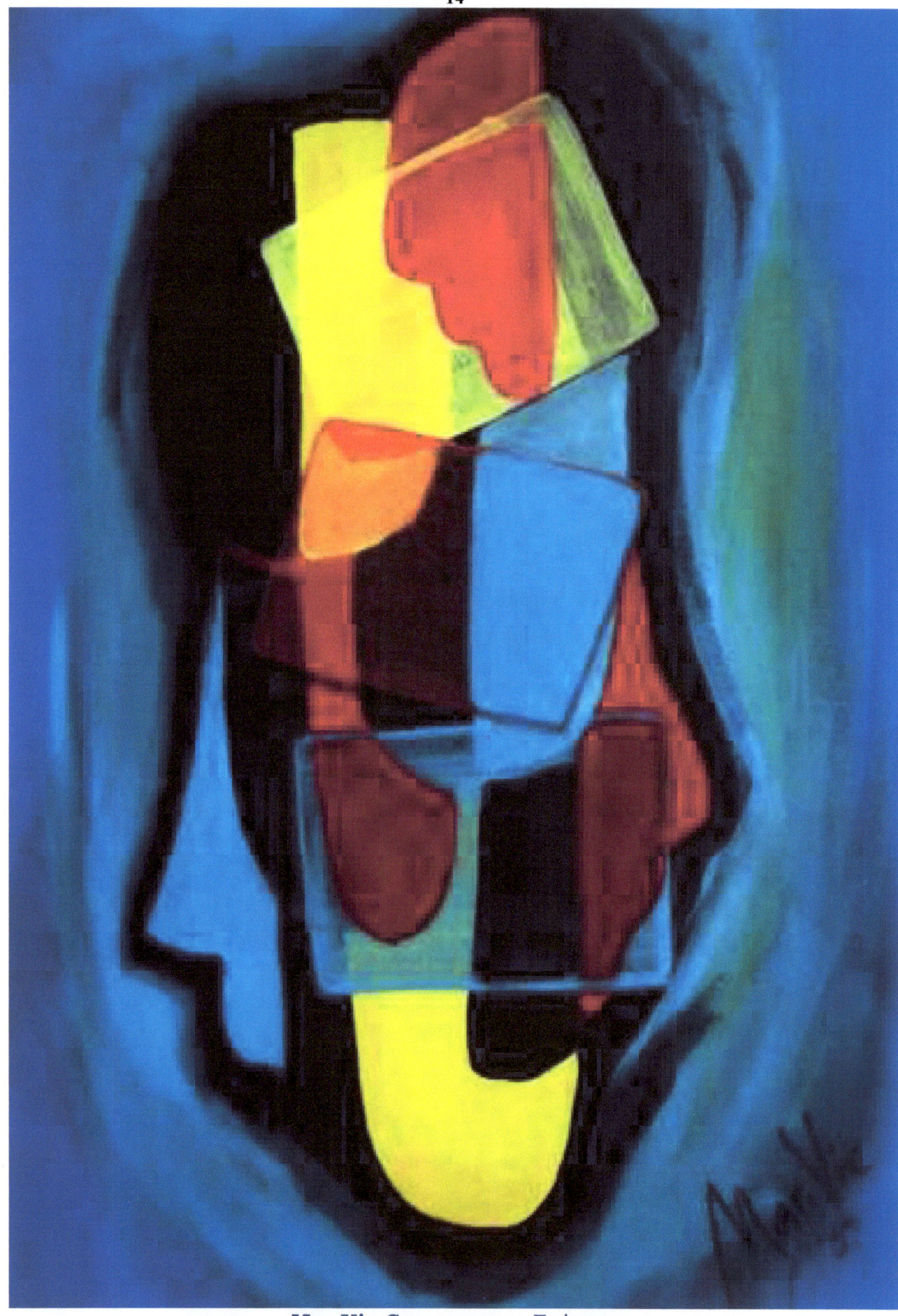

Mar-Vic Cagurangan, Enigma

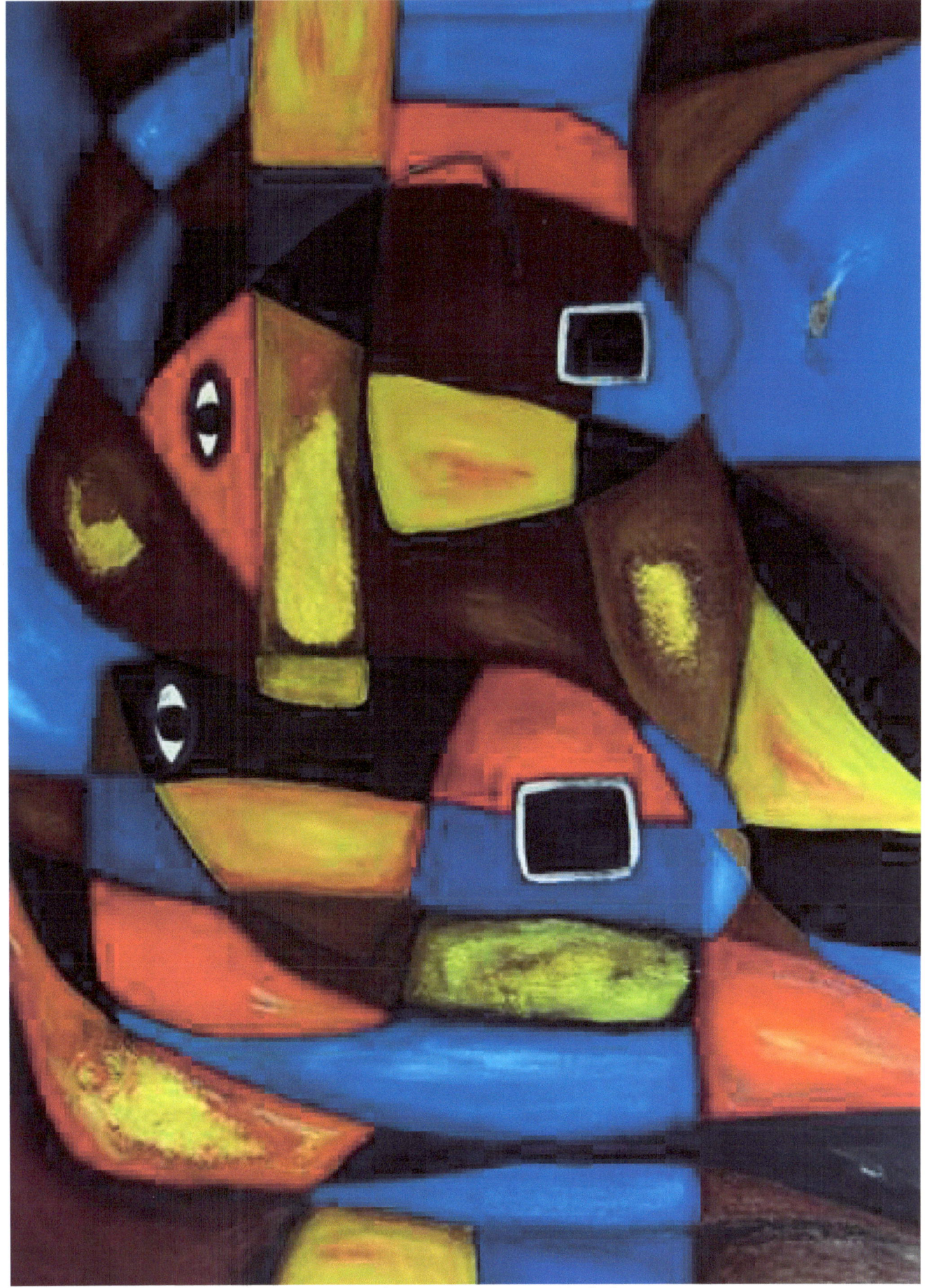

Mar-Vic Cagurangan, Weird

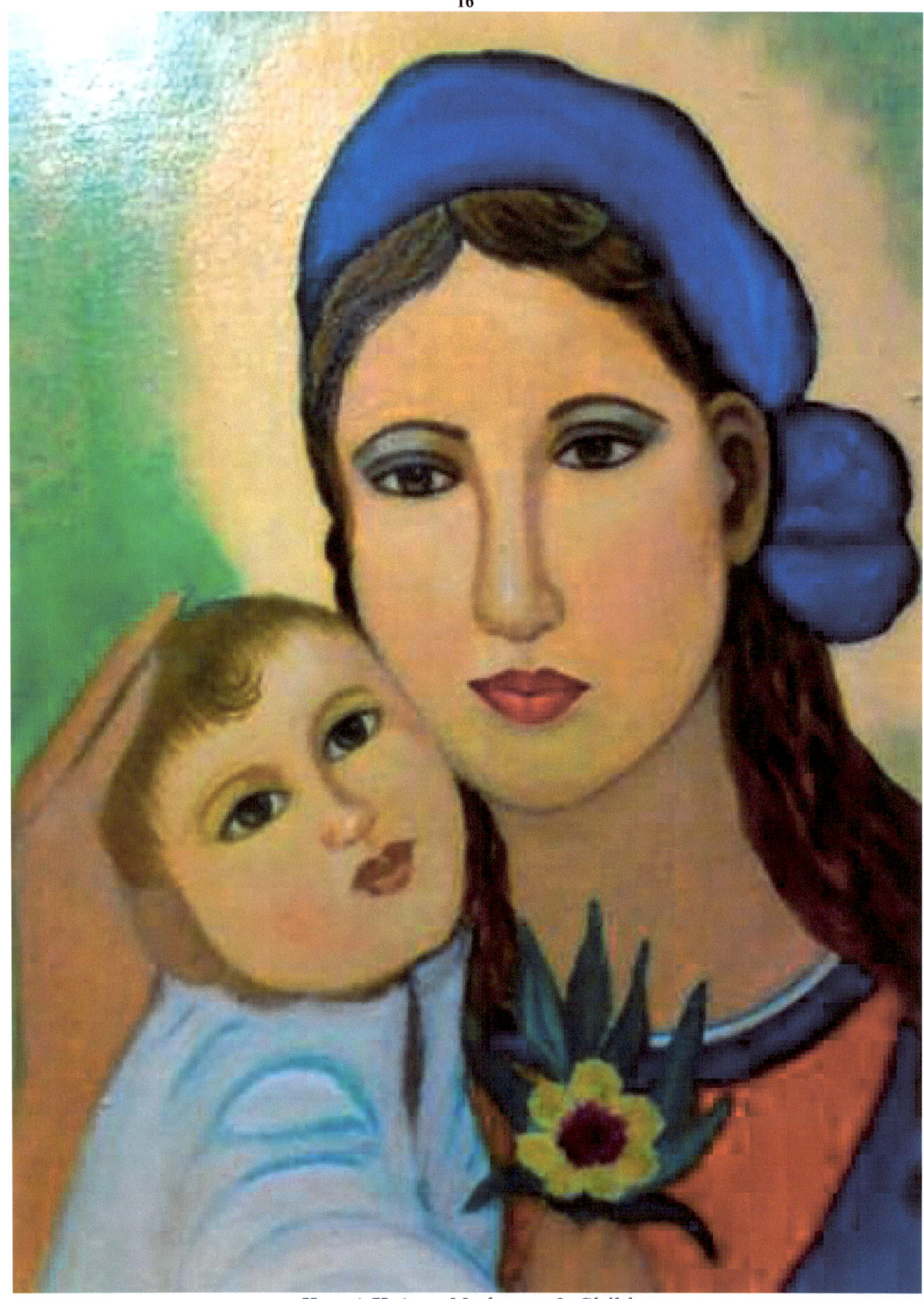

Nanet Yatco, Madonna & Child

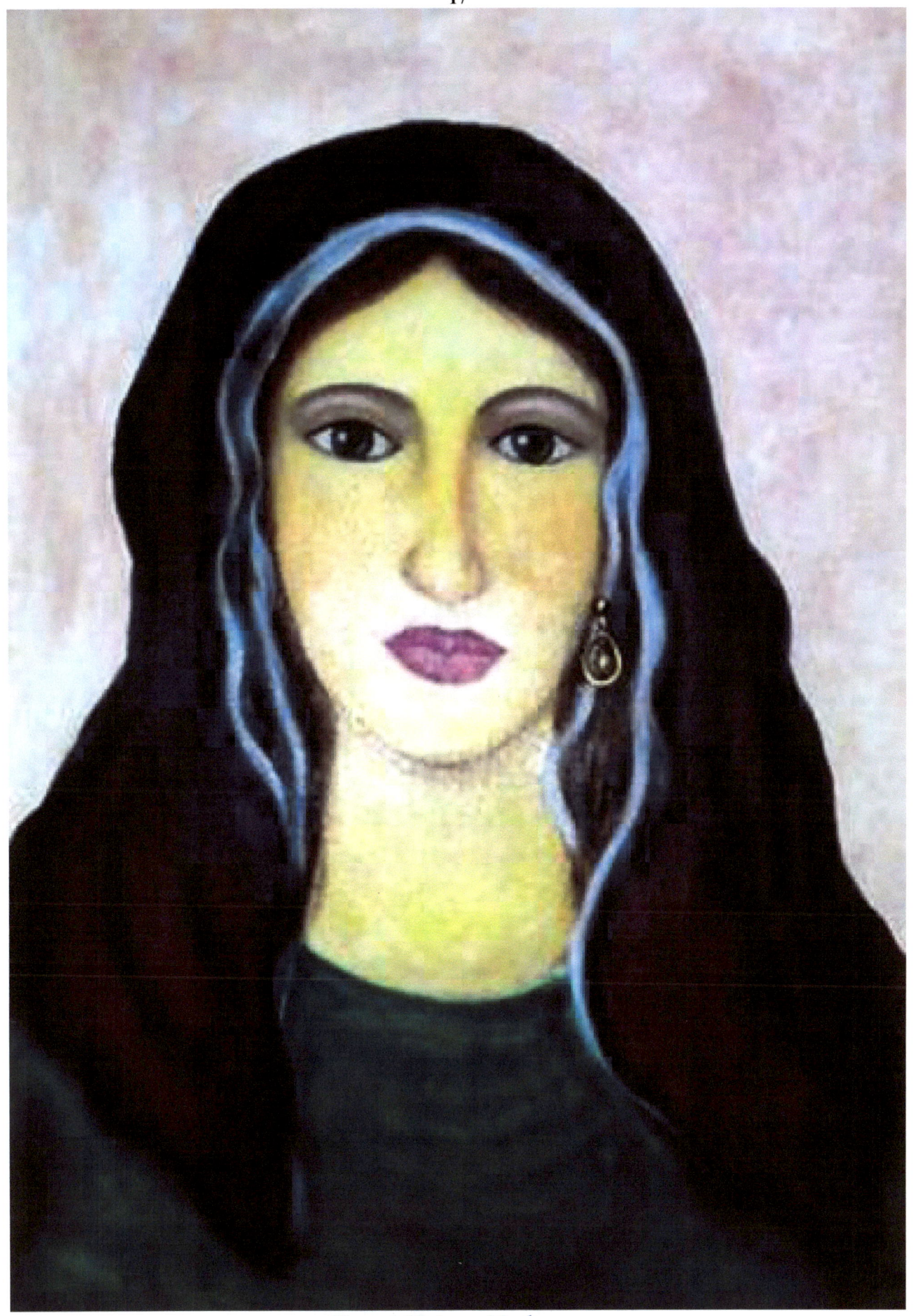

Nanet Yatco, Madonna

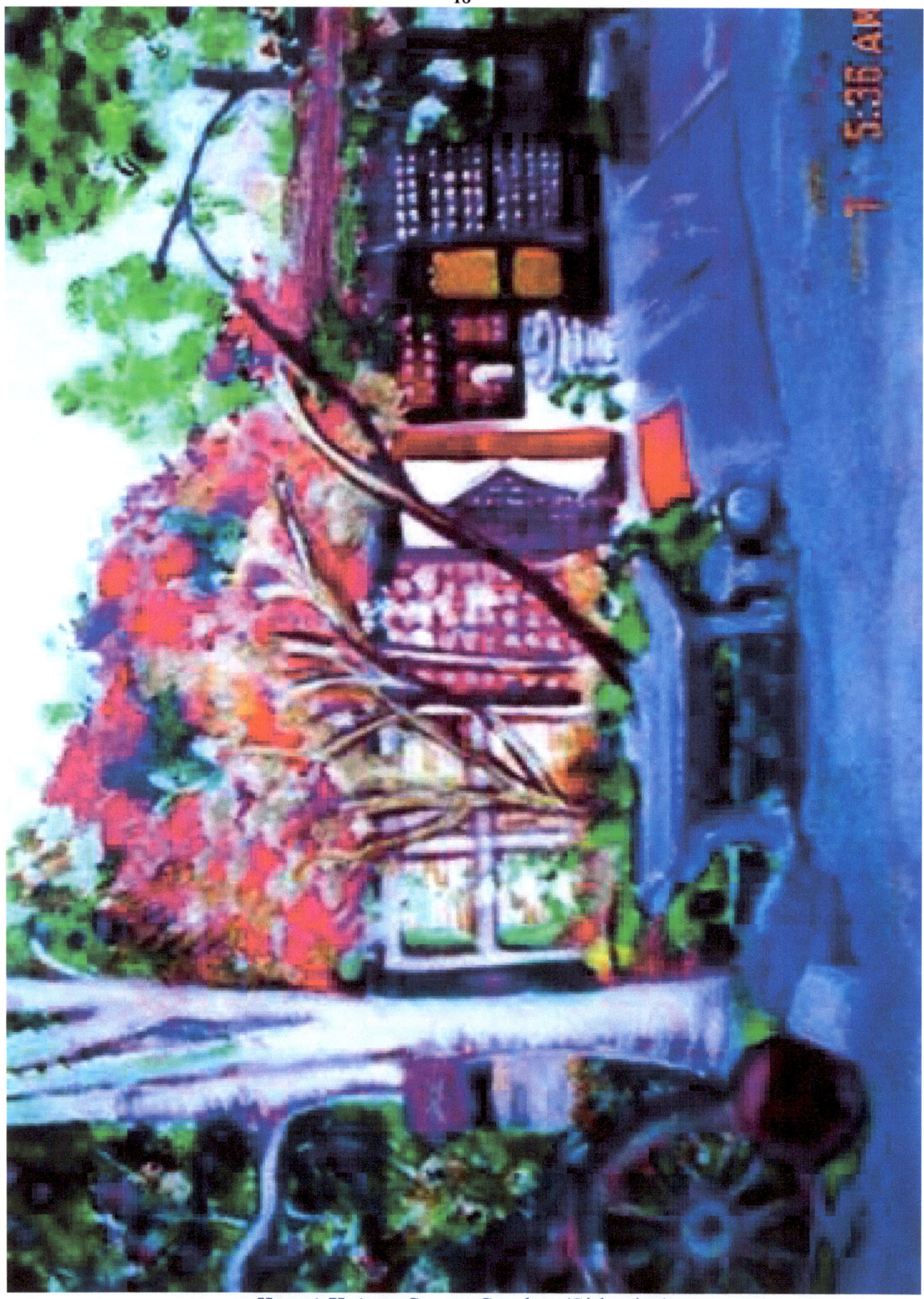

Nanet Yatco, Sonya Garden (Sidewise)

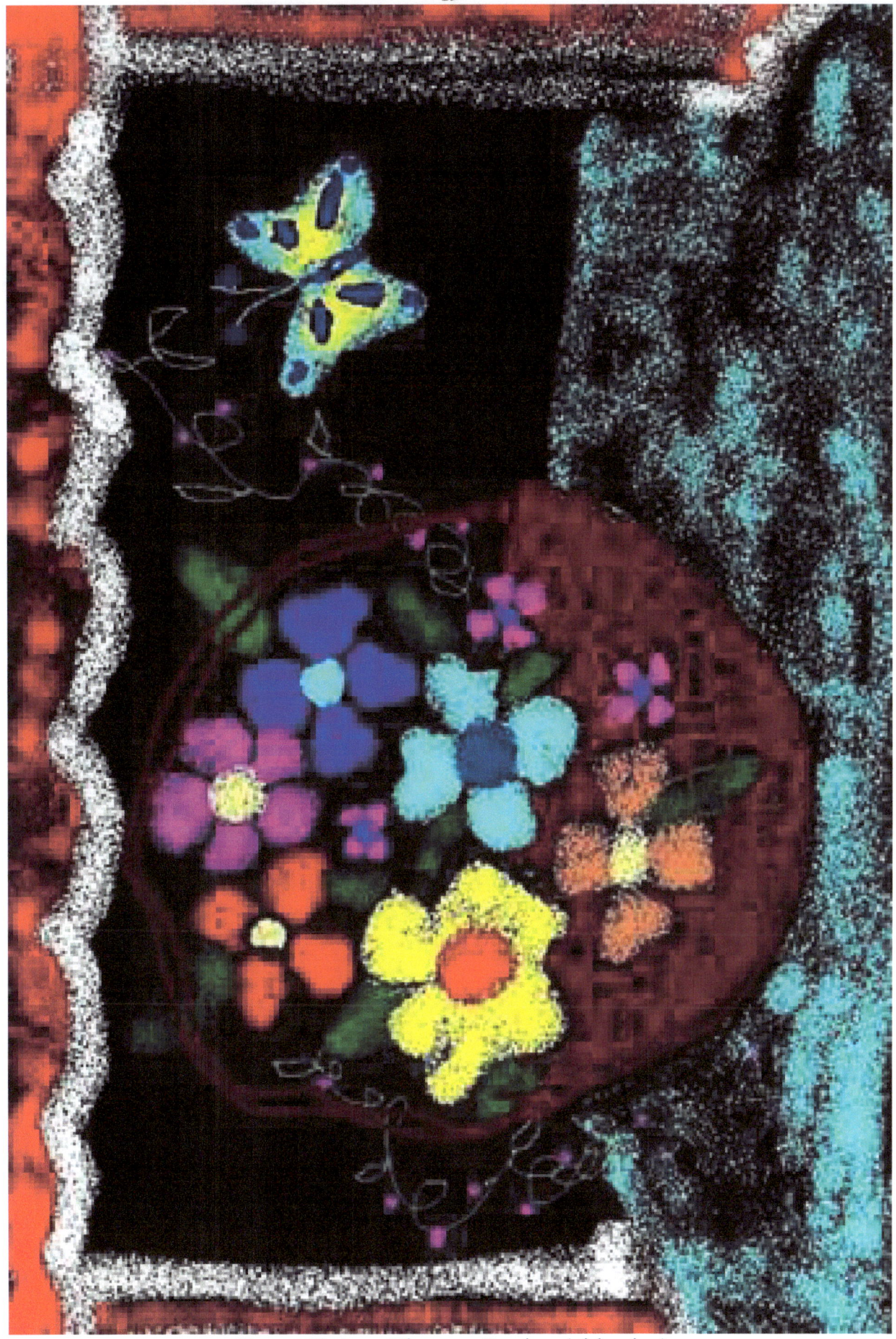

Nanet Yatco, Flowery Design (sidewise)

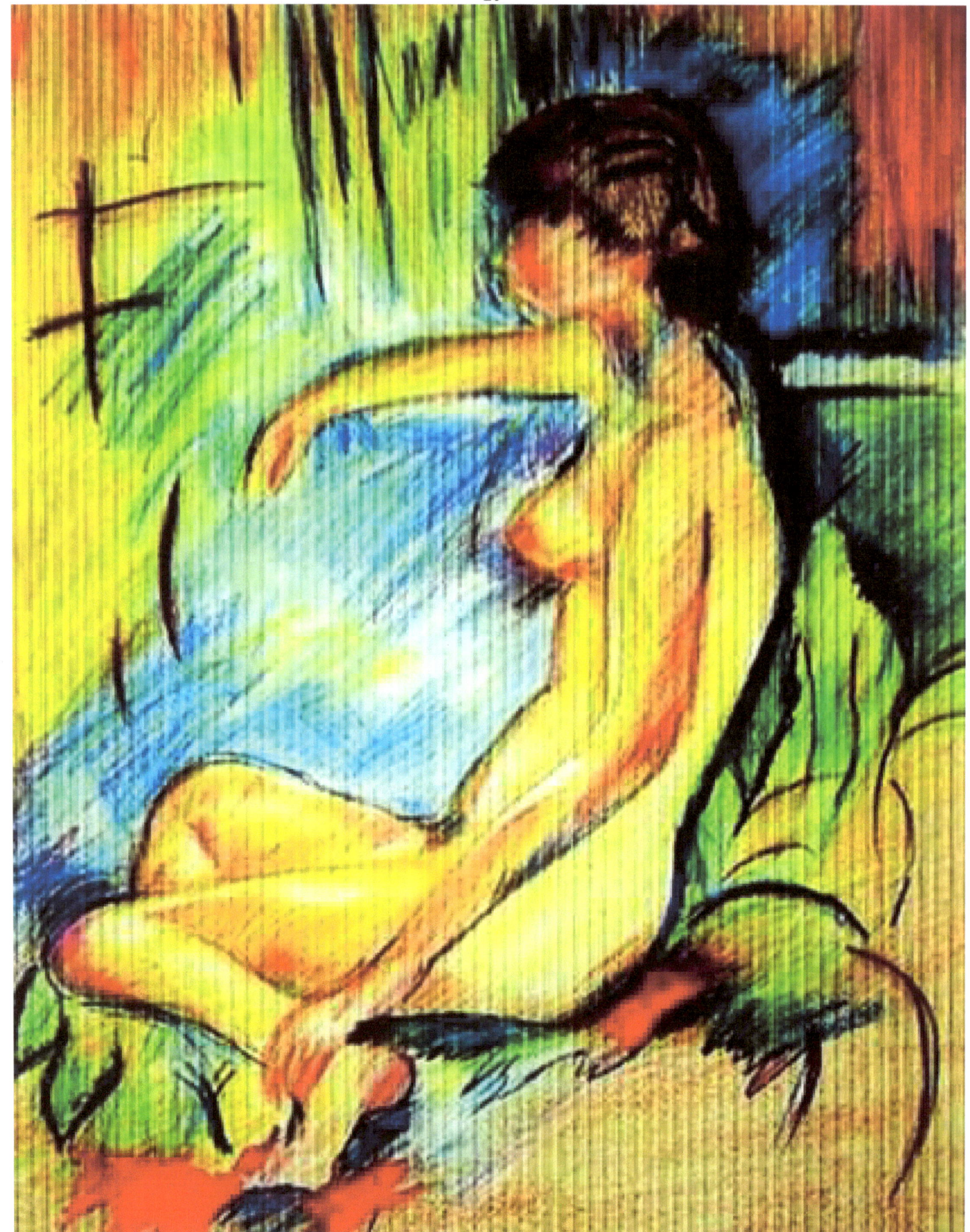

Nanet Yatco, Nude Study

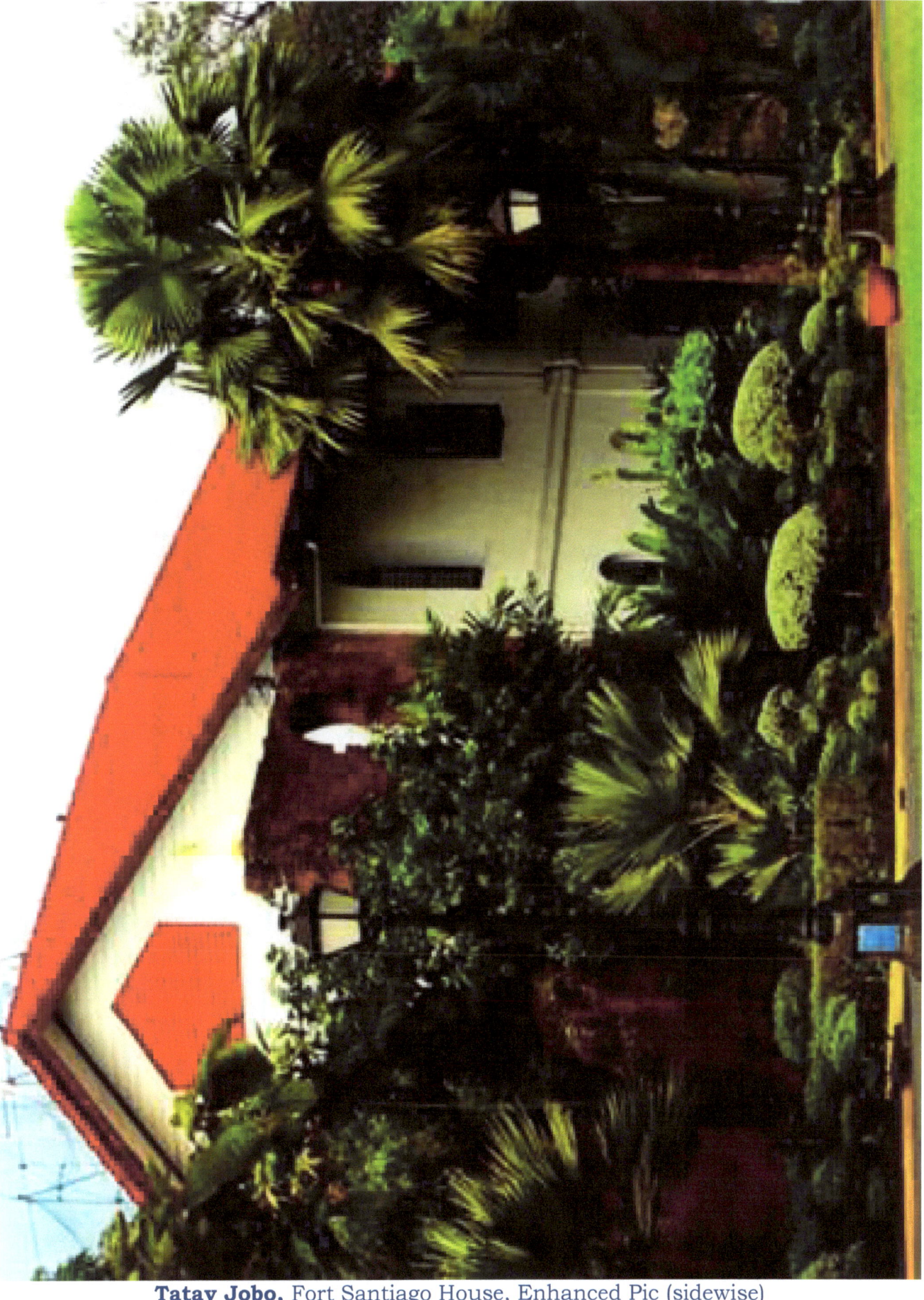

Tatay Jobo, Fort Santiago House, Enhanced Pic (sidewise)

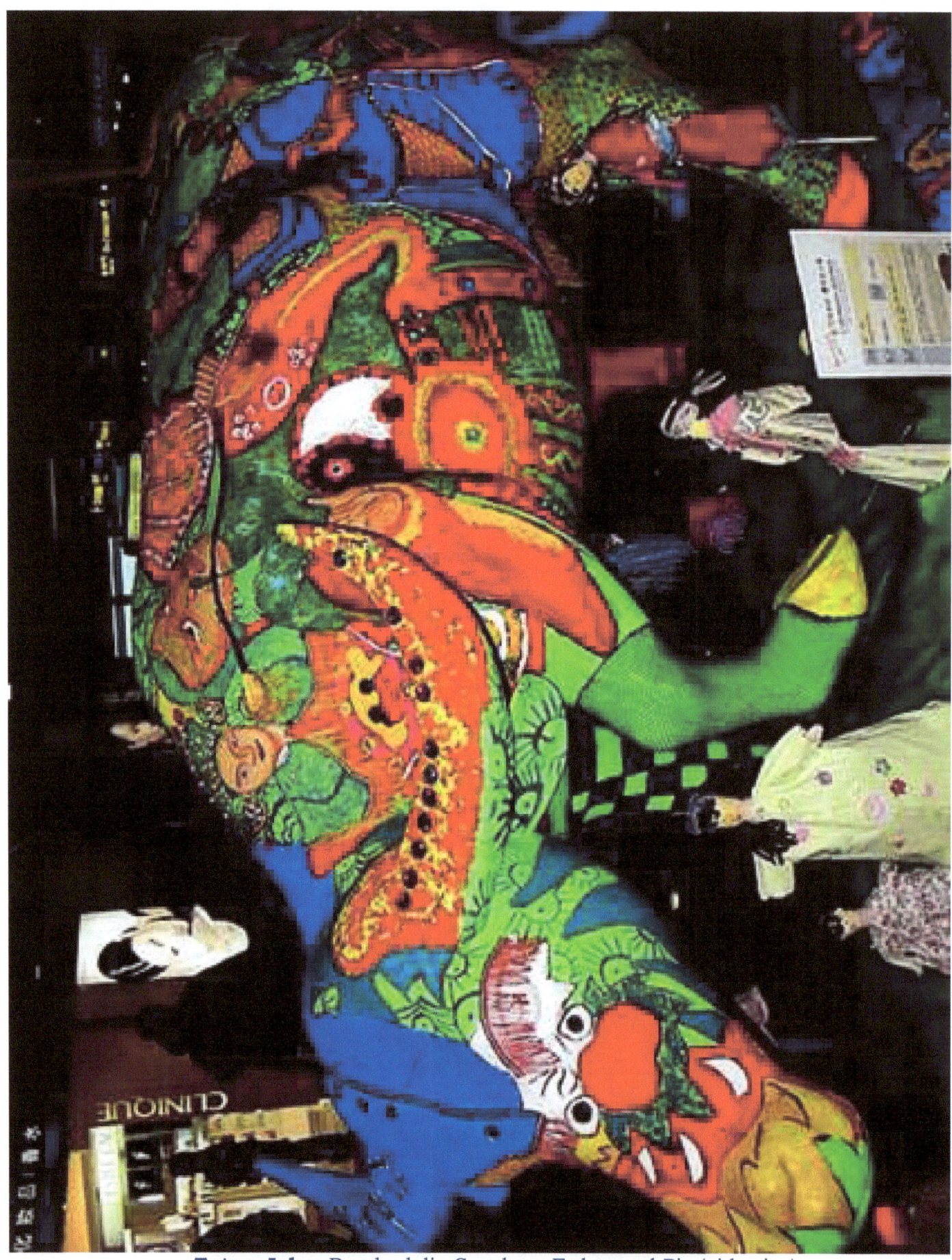

Tatay Jobo, Psychedelic Carabao, Enhanced Pic (sidewise)

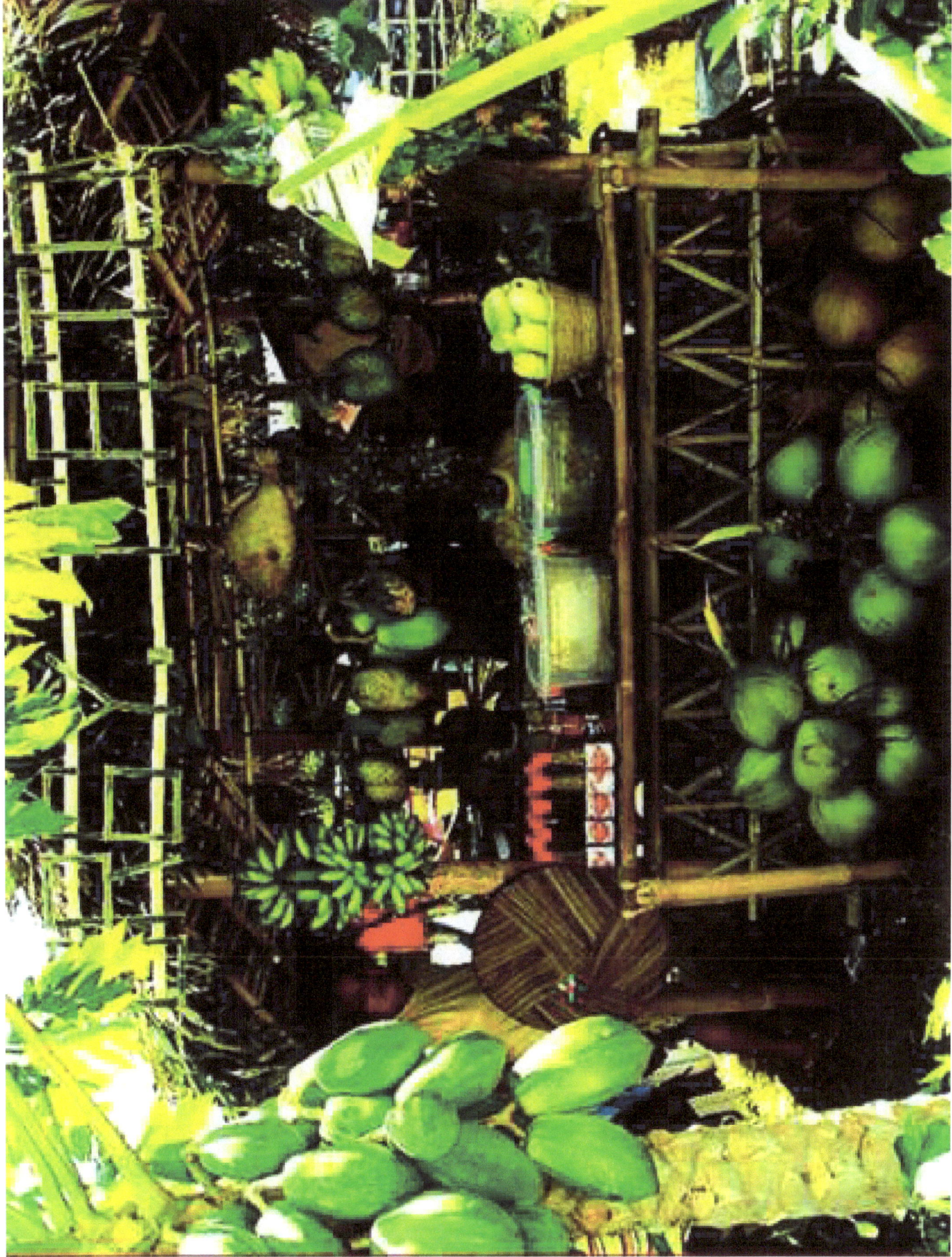

Tatay Jobo, Fruit Stand, Enhanced Pic (sidewise)

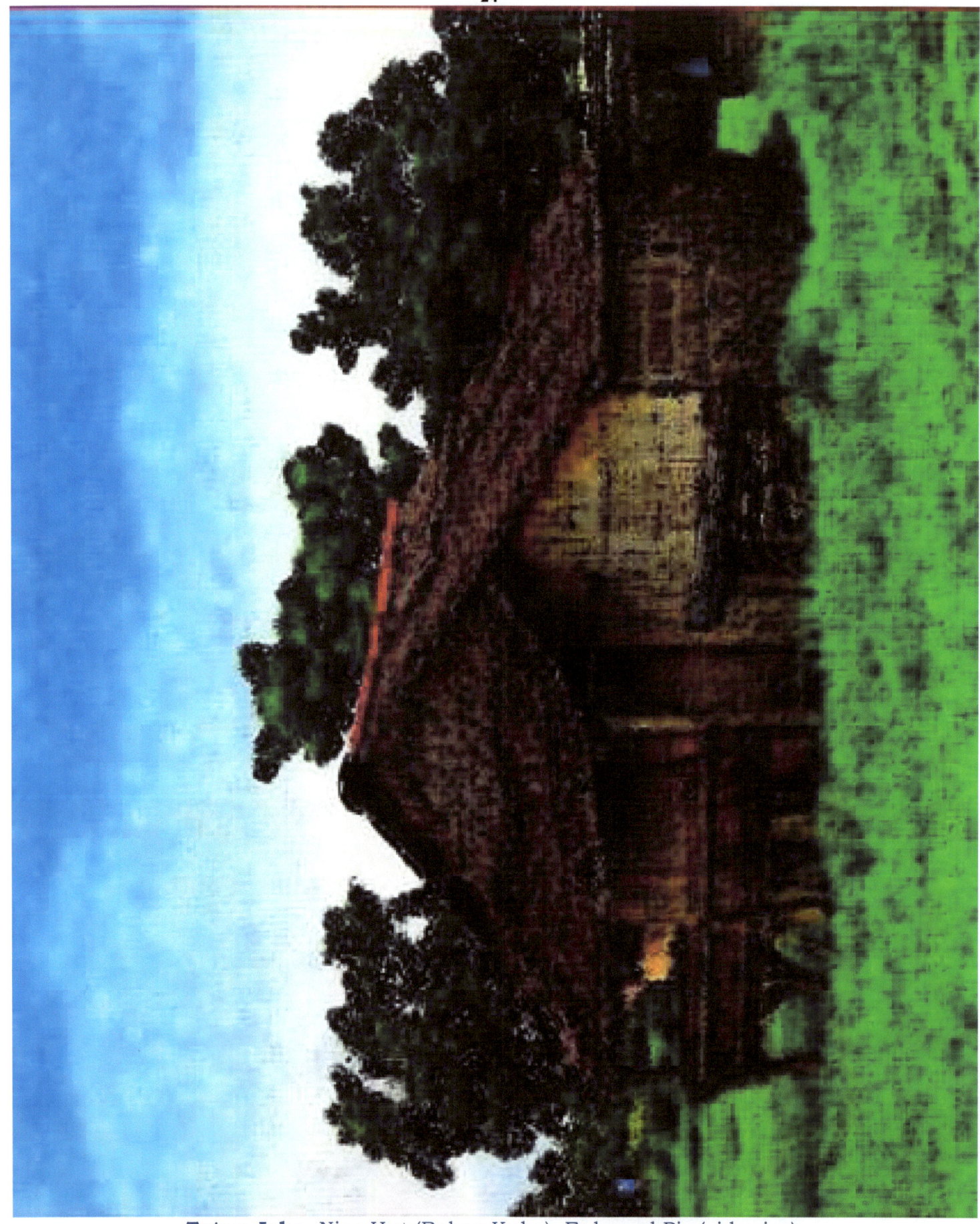

Tatay Jobo, Nipa Hut (Bahay Kubo), Enhaned Pic (sidewise)

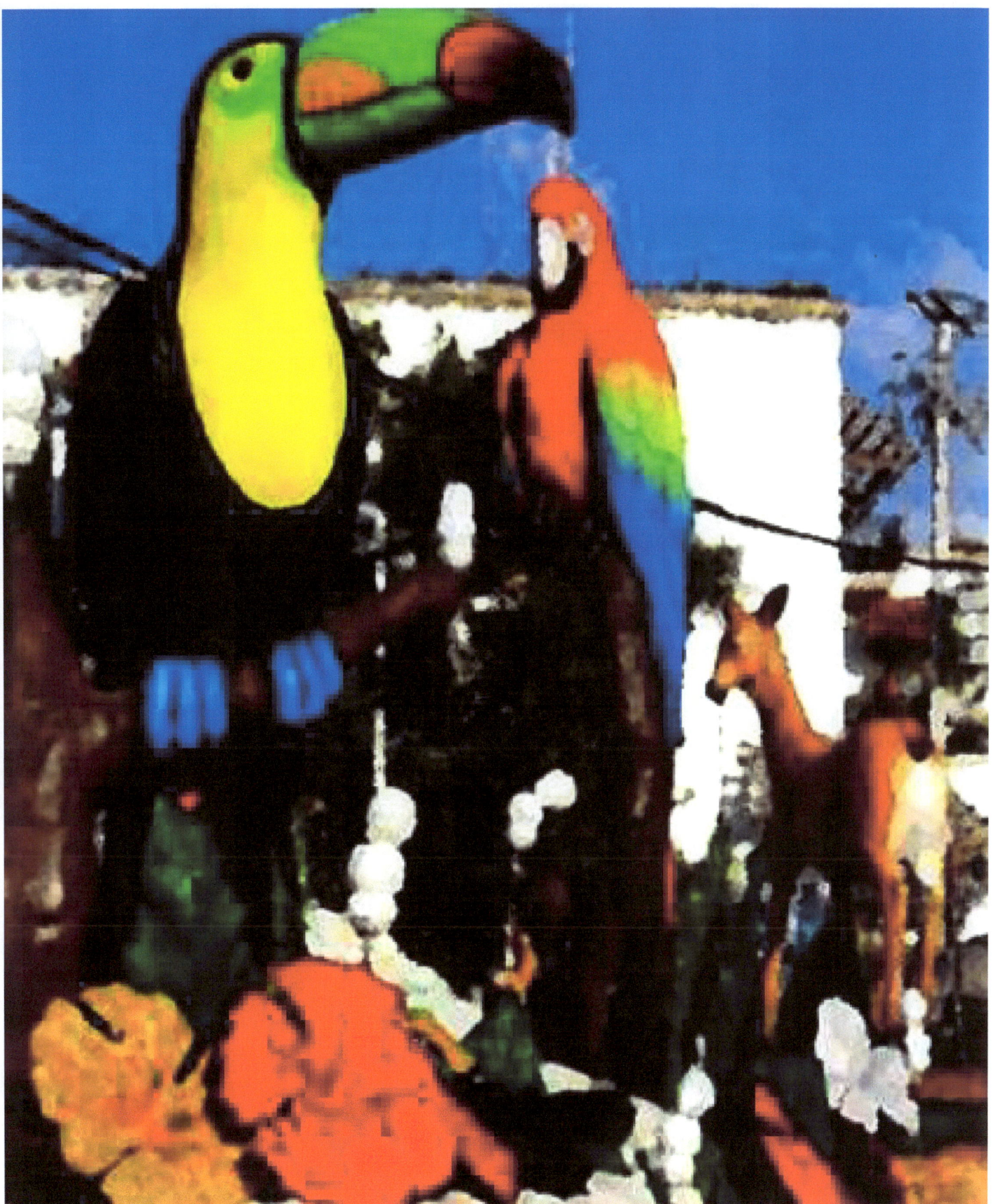

Tatay Jobo, Parrots, Enhanced Pic

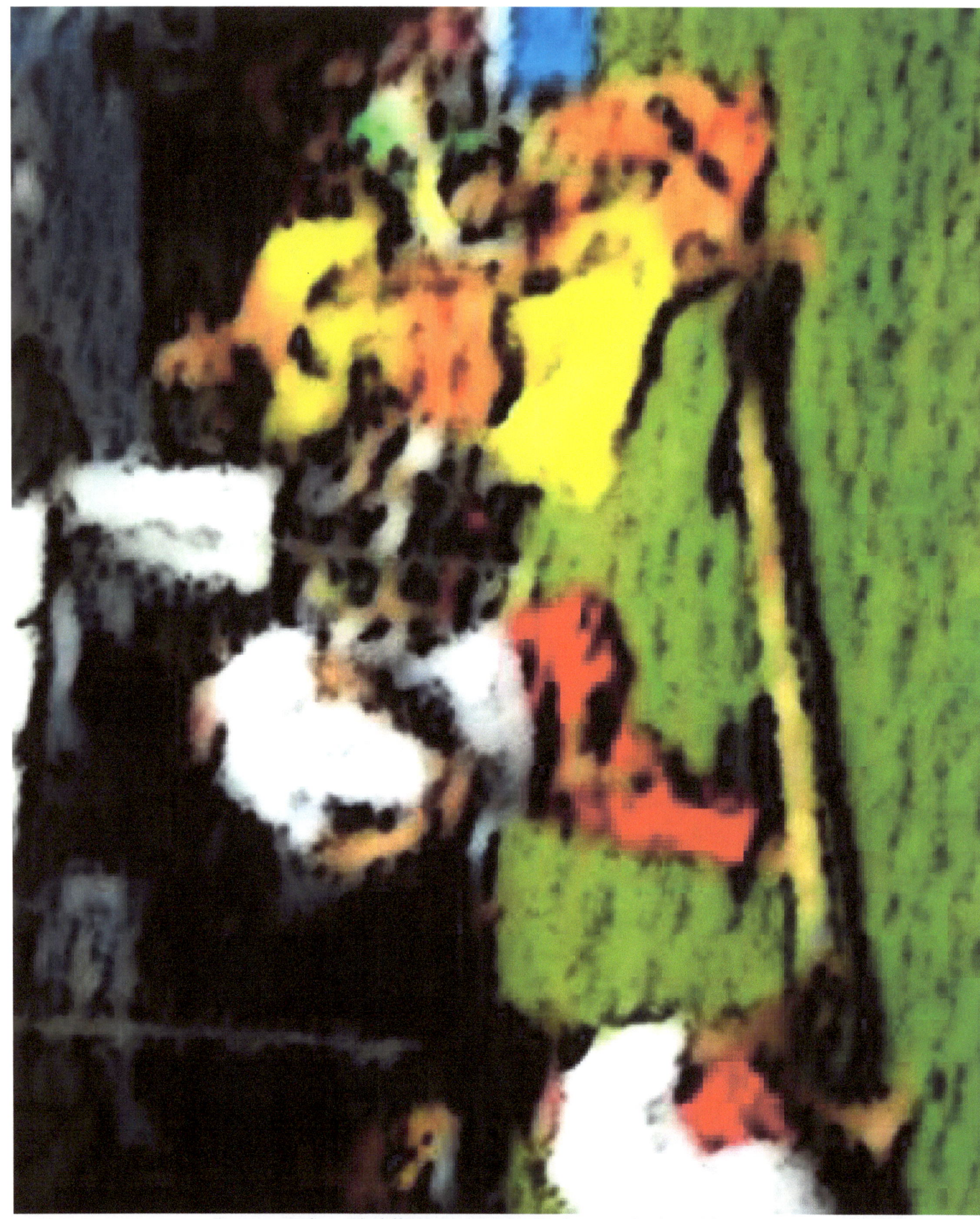

Tatay Jobo, Tinkling Dancers, Enhanced Pic (sidewise)

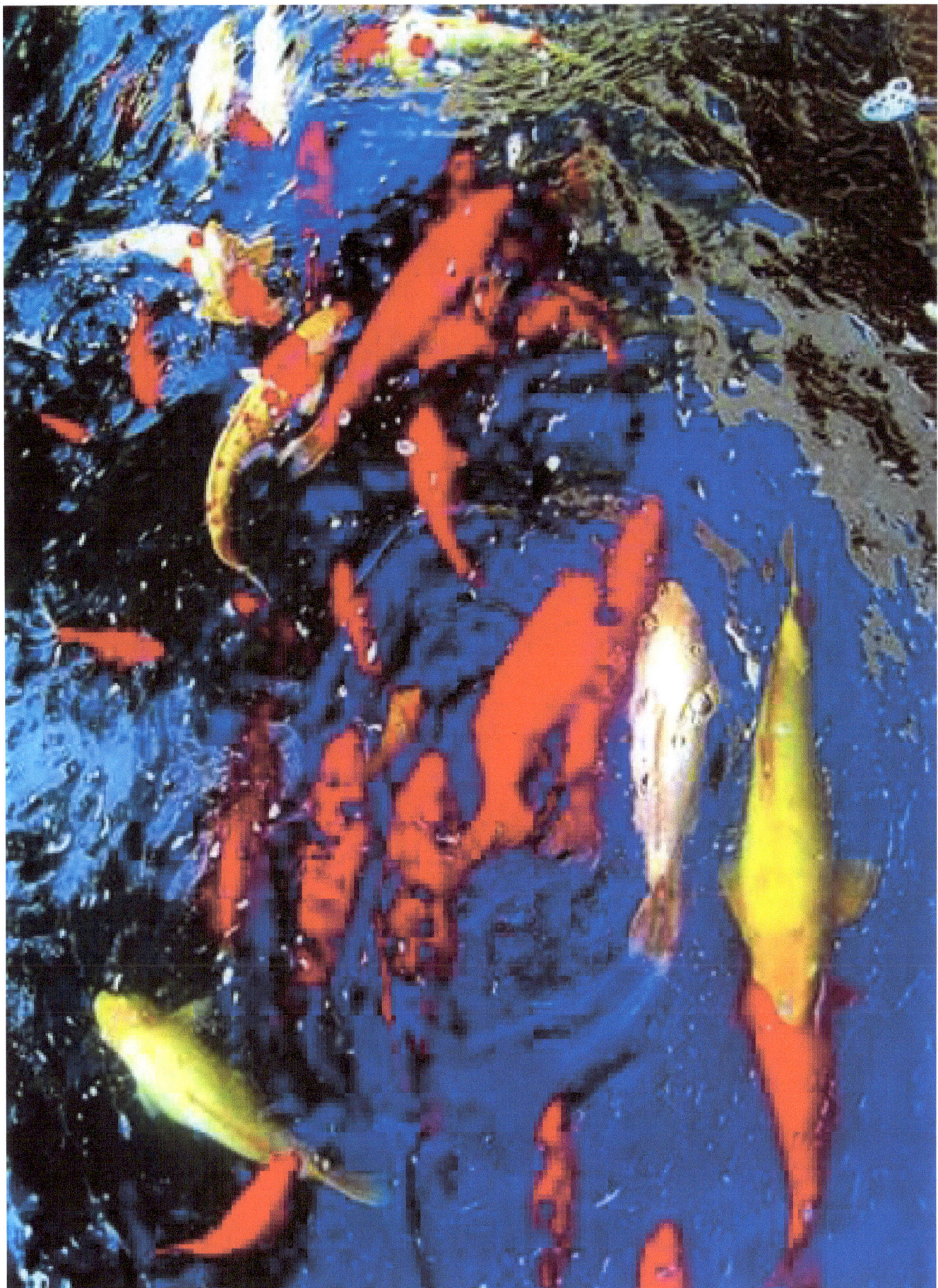

Tatay Jobo, Pool Fishes, Enhanced Pic (sidewise)

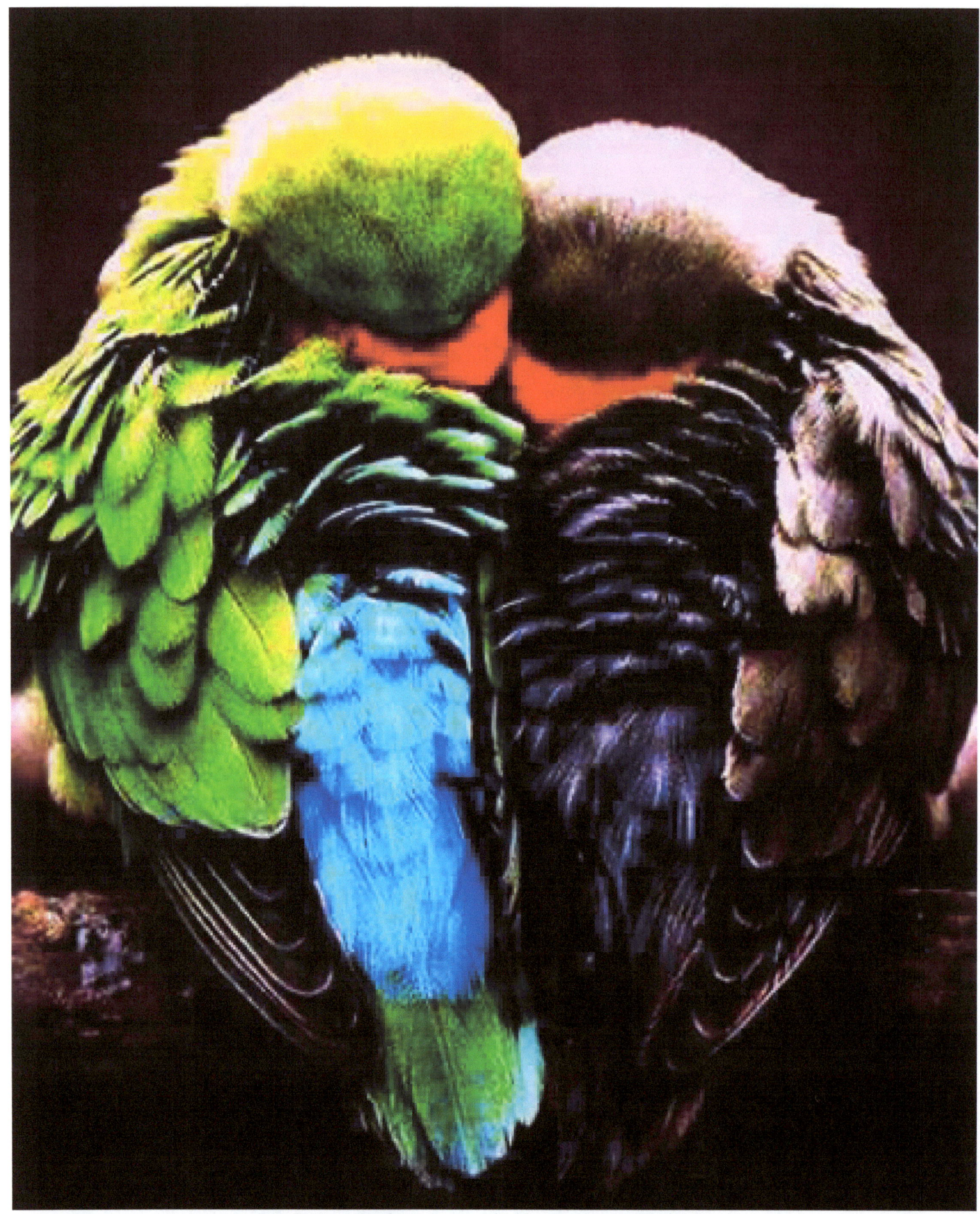

Tatay Jobo, Love Birds, Enhanced Pic

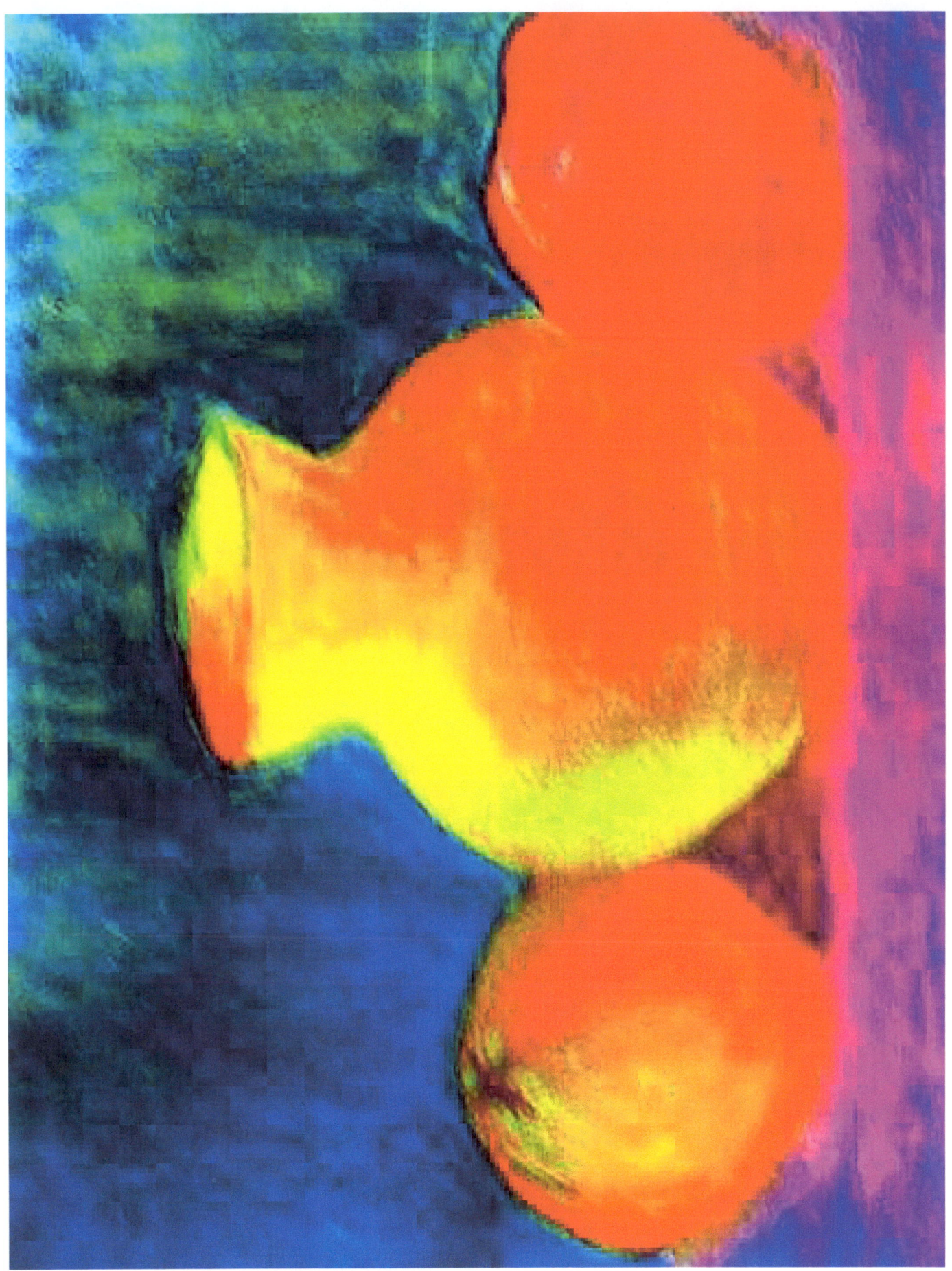

Loleng Liwanag, Jar and Fruits

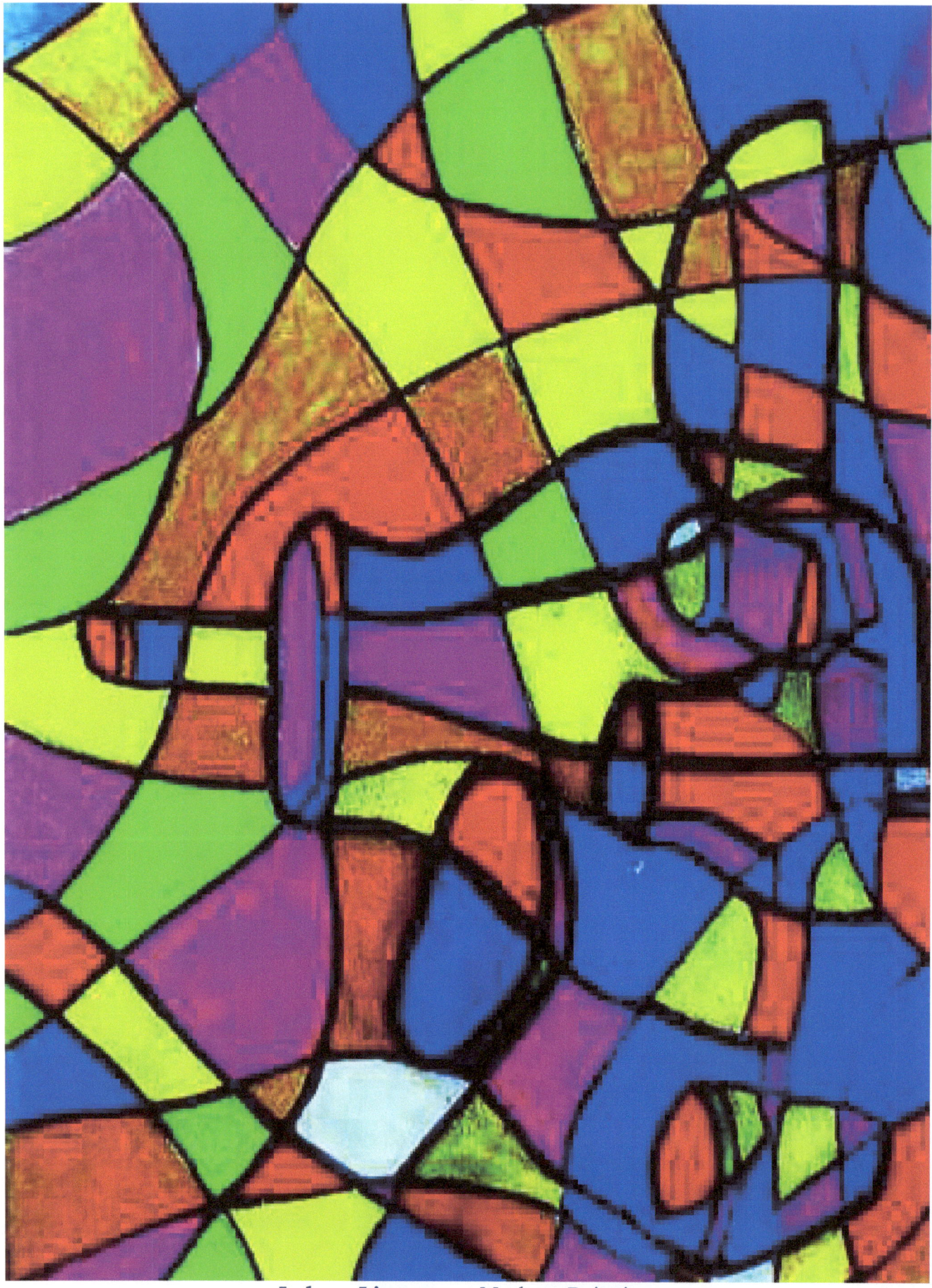

Loleng Liwanag, Modern Painting

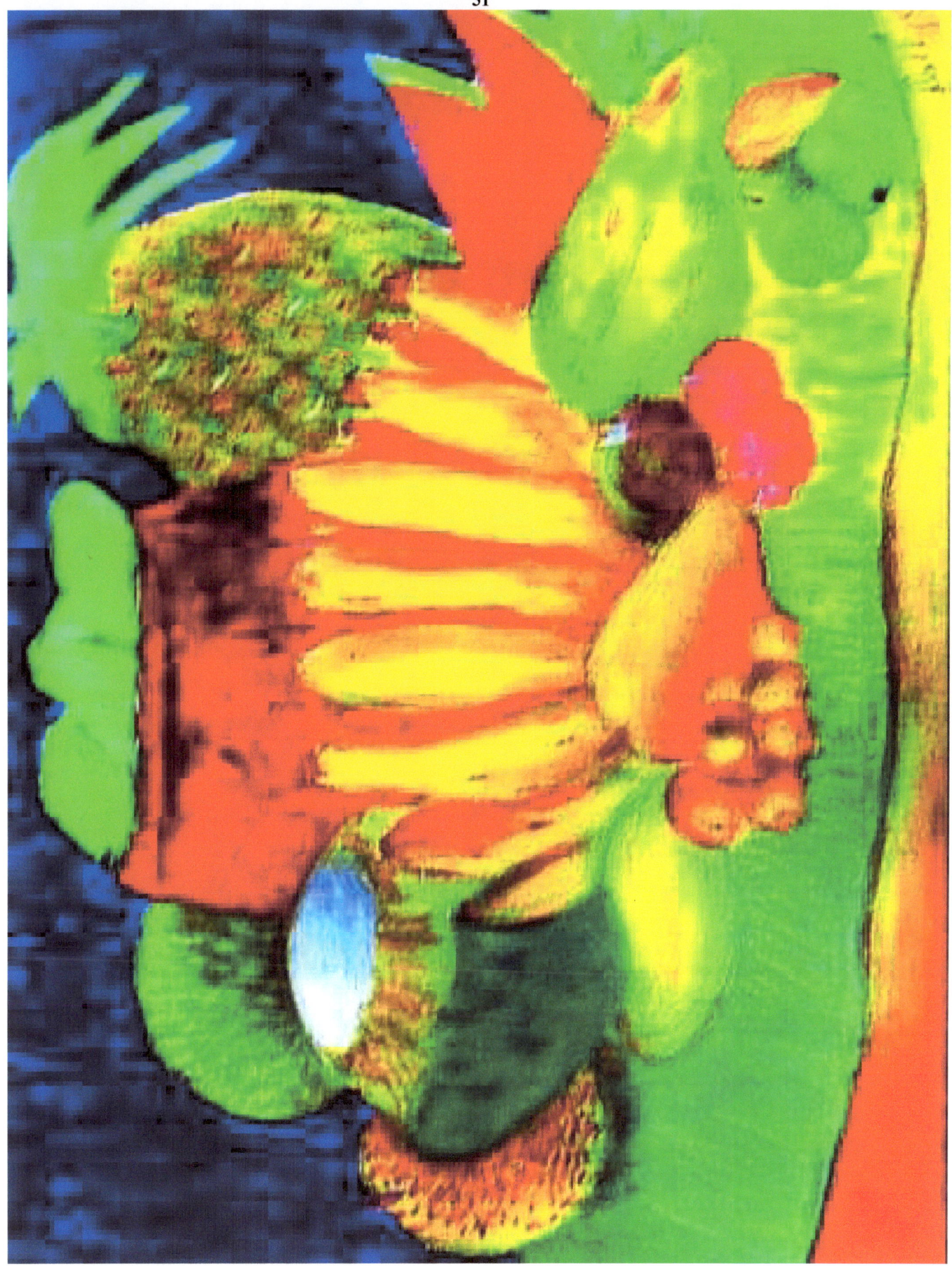

Loleng Liwanag, Bananas + Other Fruits, Still (sidewise)

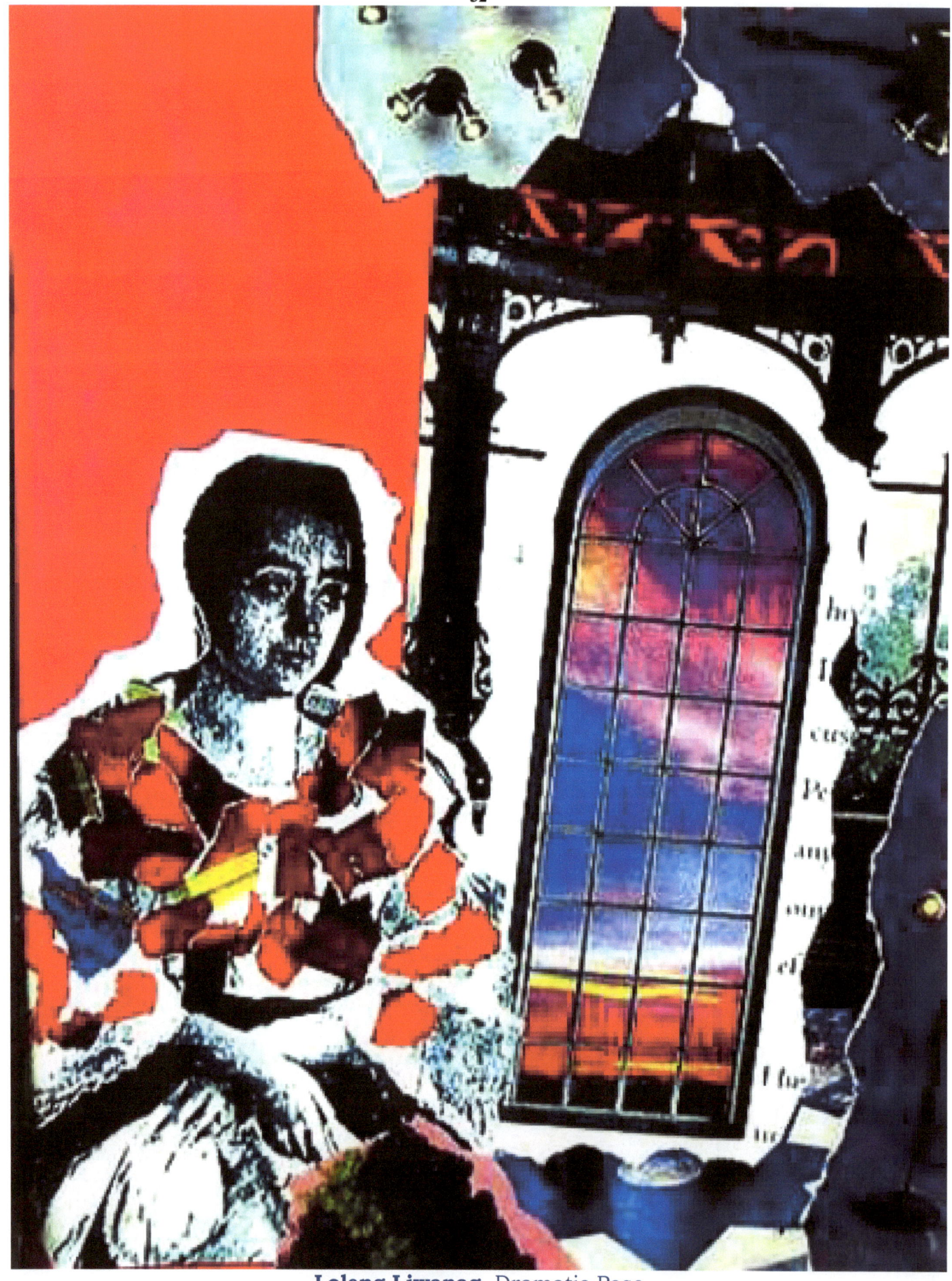

Loleng Liwanag, Dramatic Pose

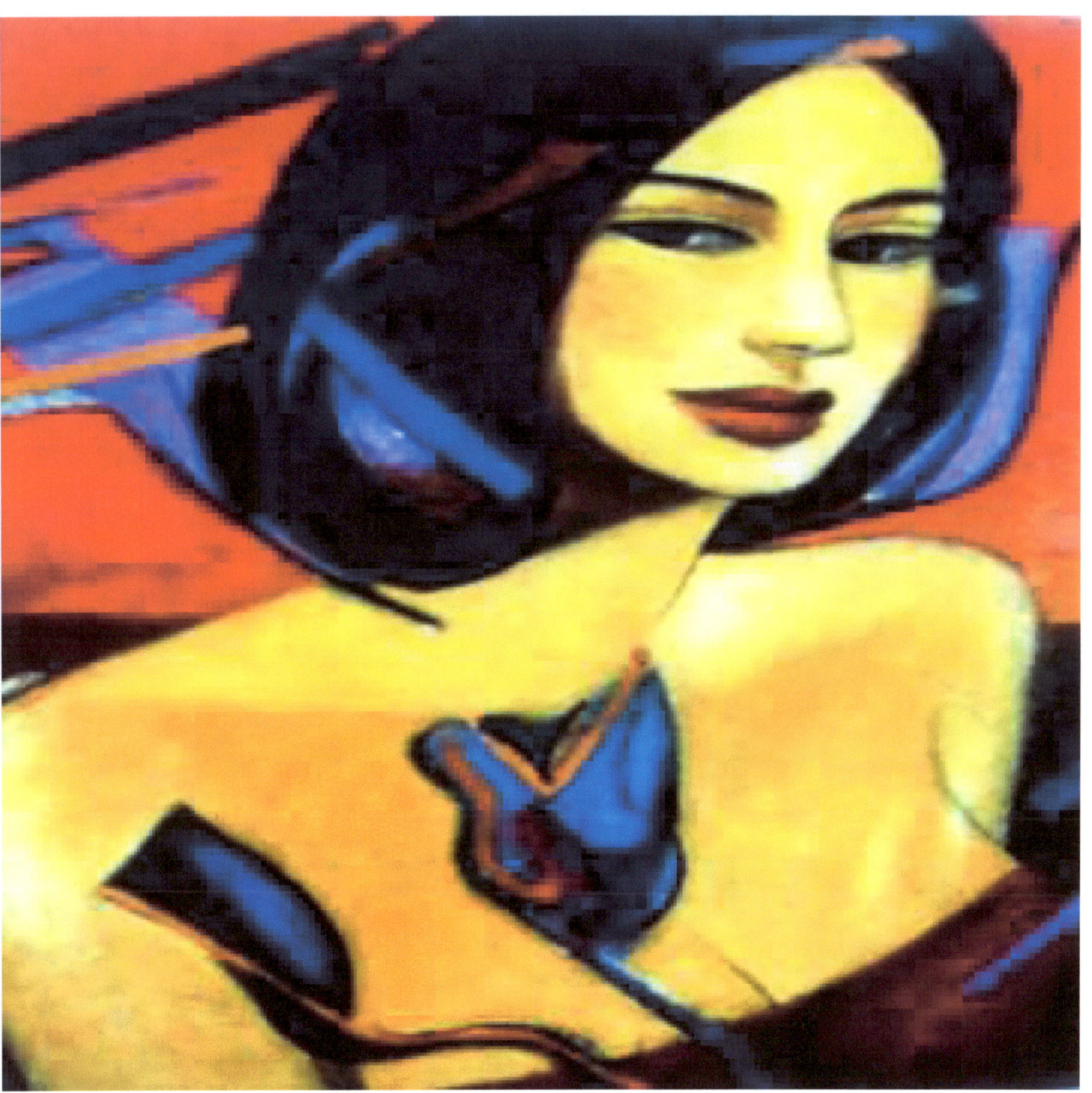

Hermes Alegre, Cute Face

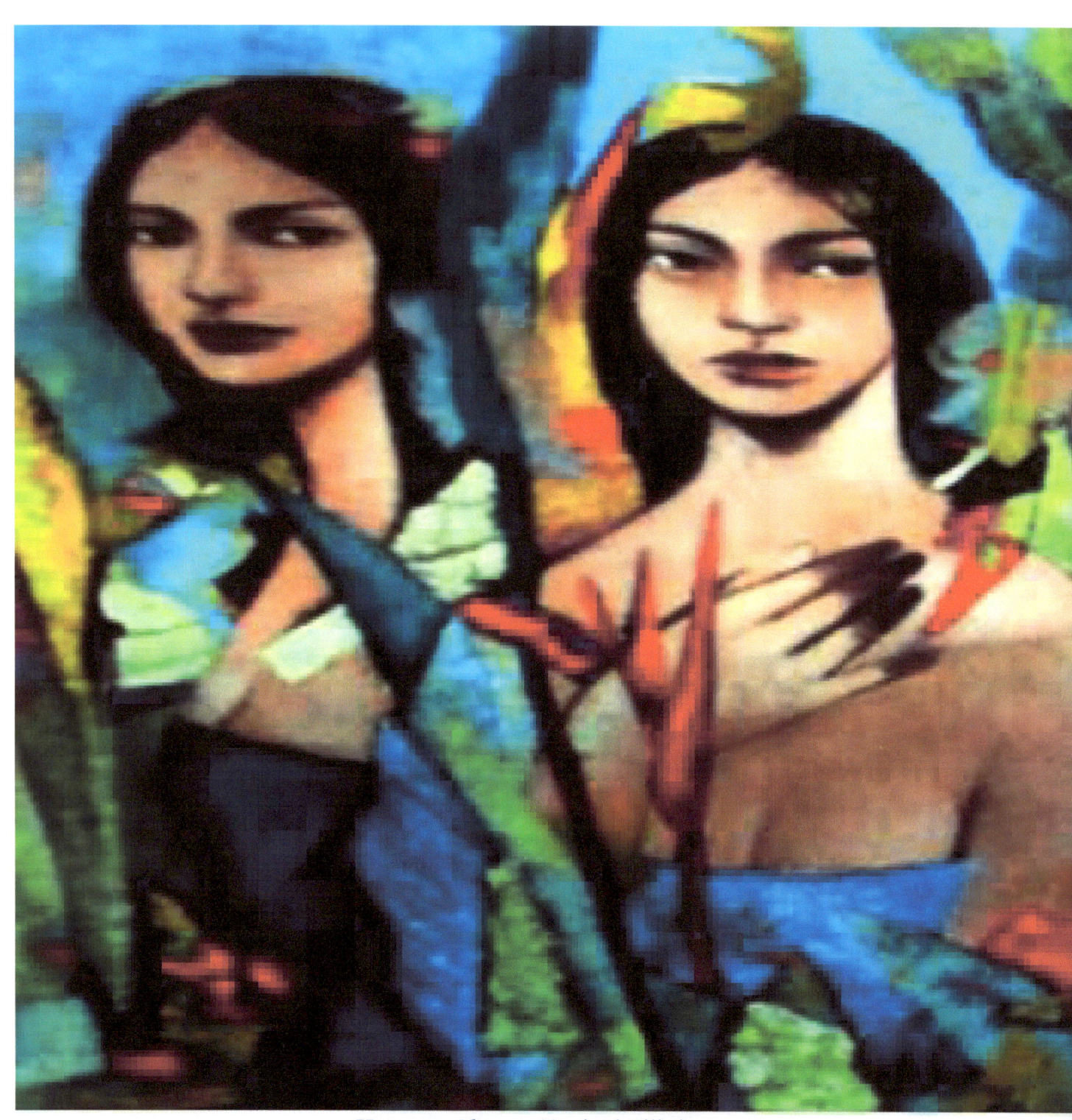

Hermes Alegre, Typical Filipinas

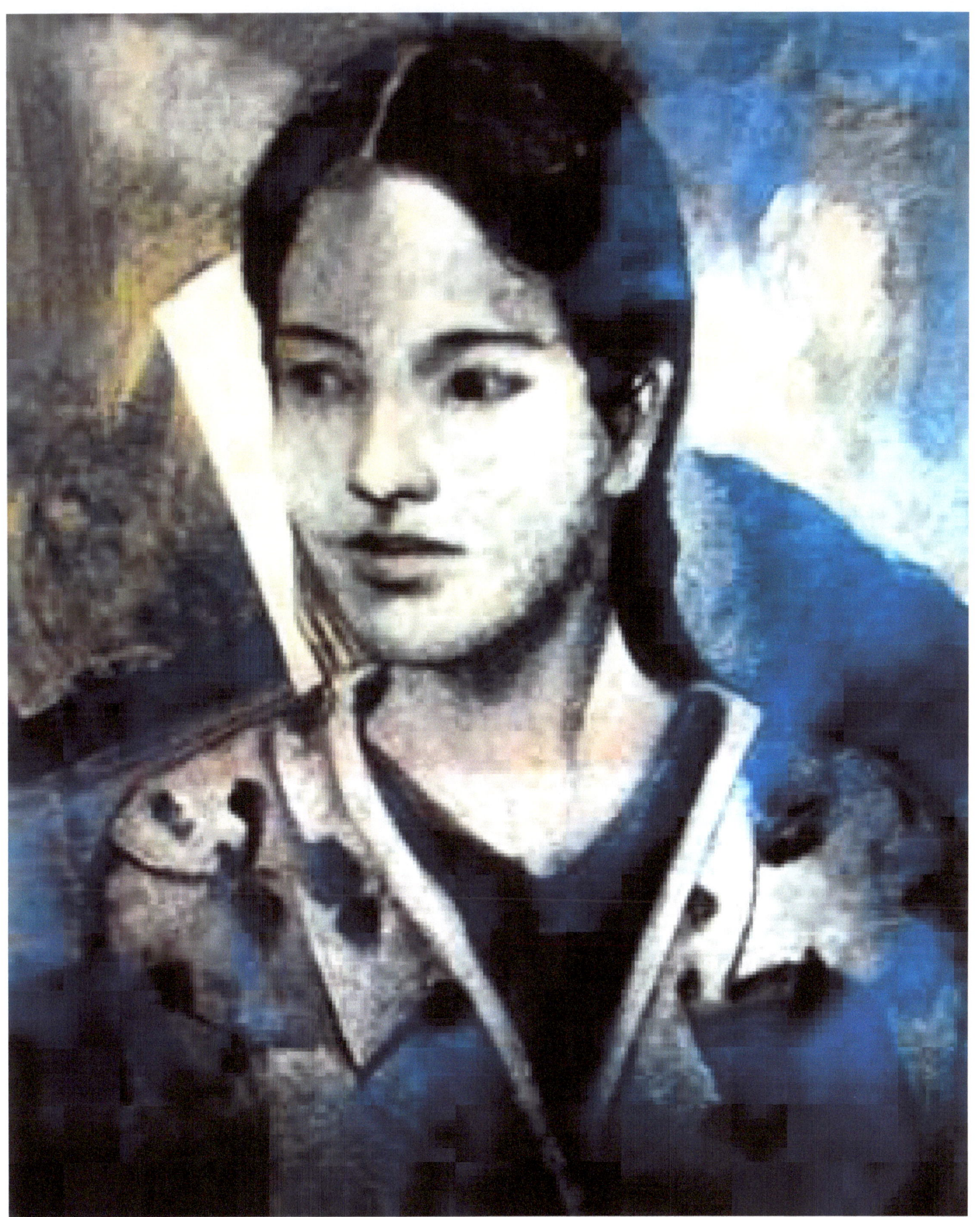

Hermes Alegre, School Girl Look

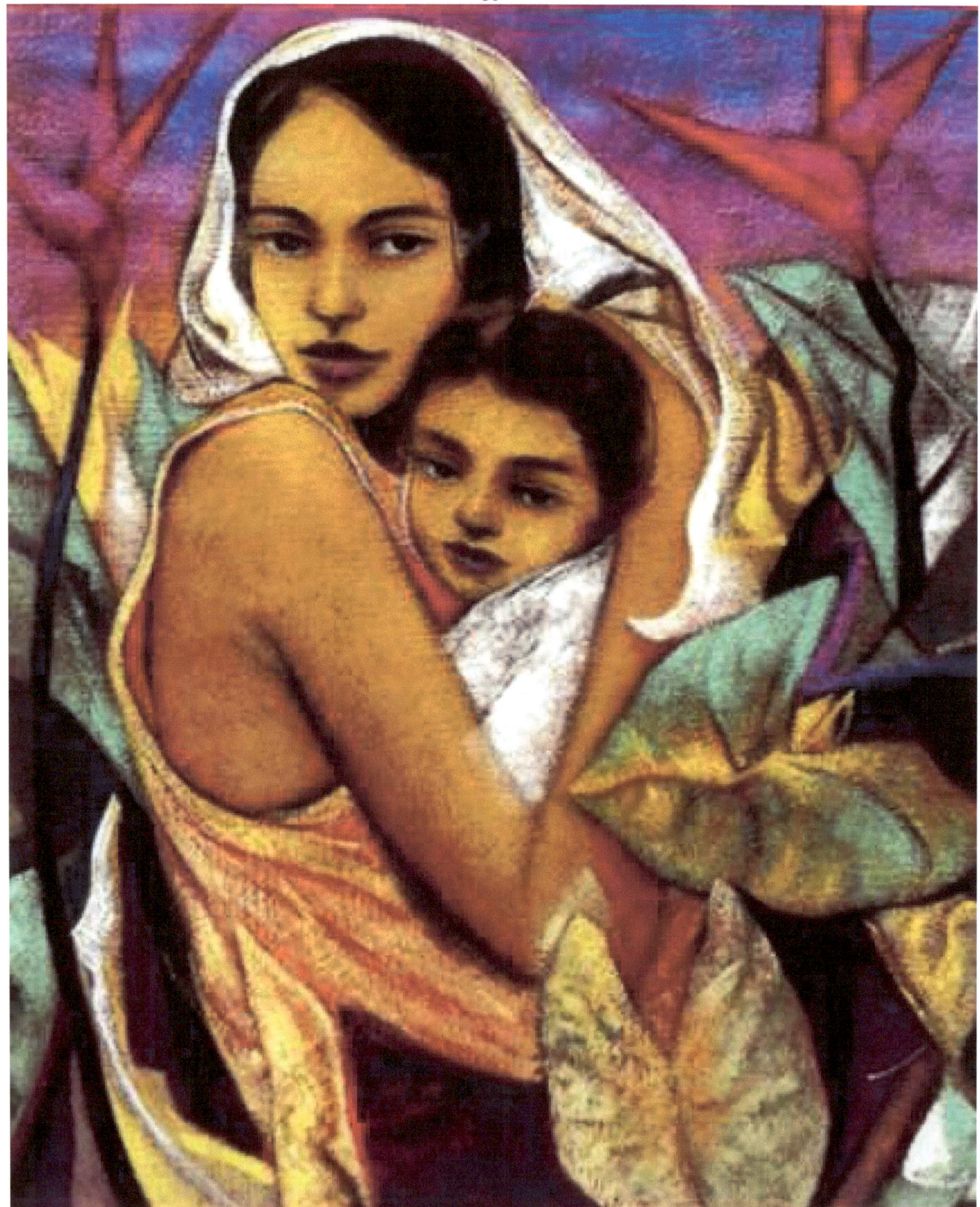

Hermes Alegre, Rural Modonna & Child

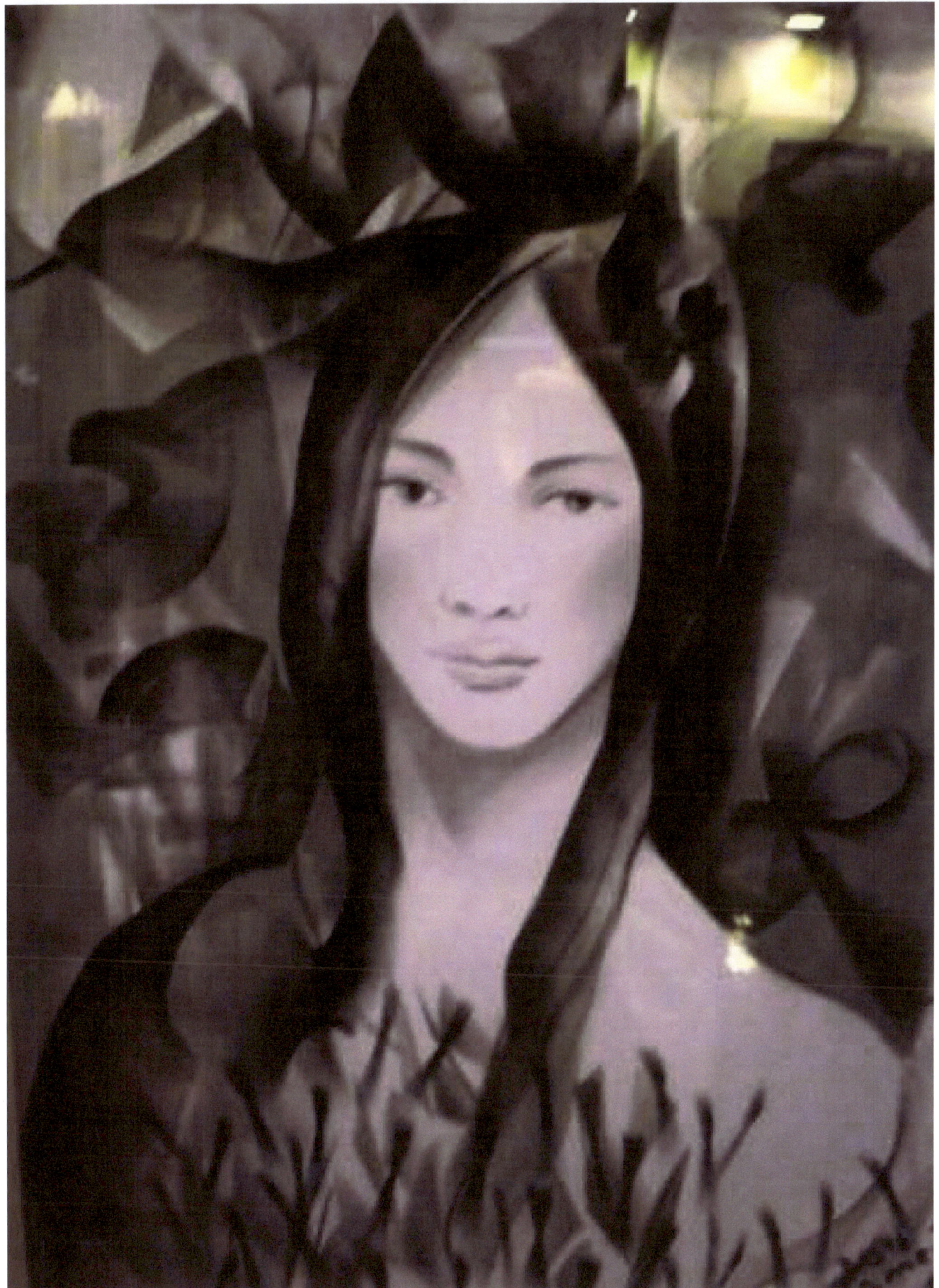

Hermes Alegre, Chinita Girl

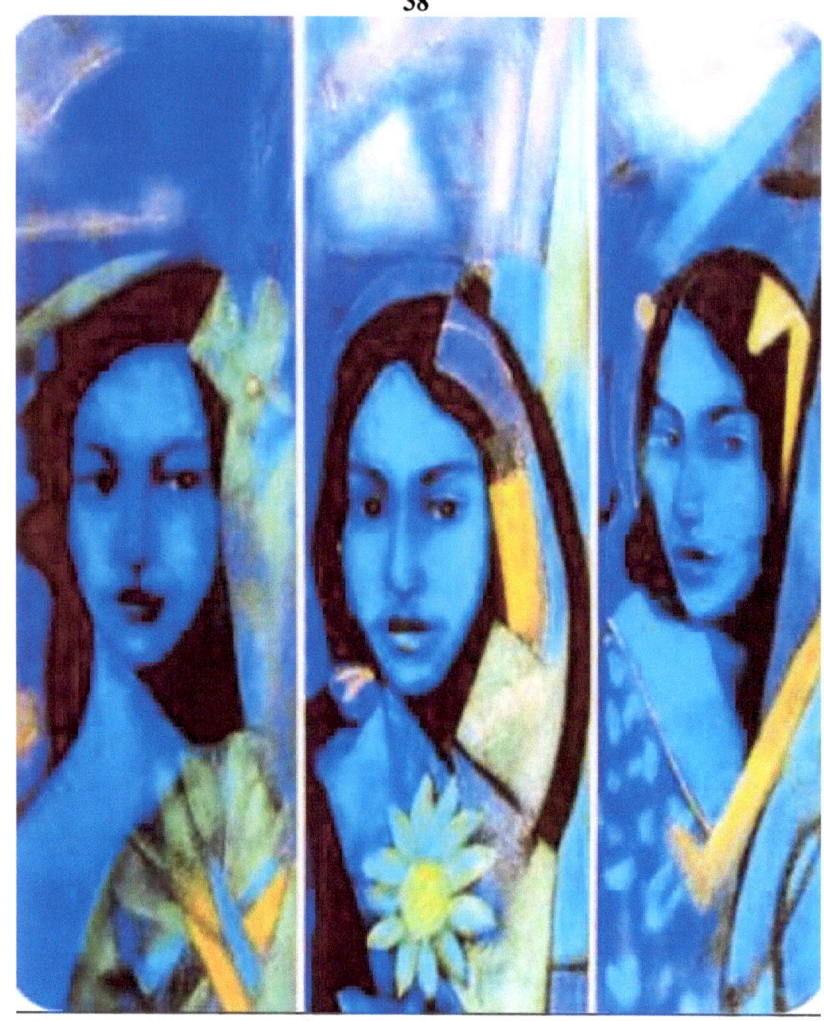

Hermes Alegre, Three Lovely Faces

Self-Publisher's List - Other Books

Writings 1 Book, 2009 + I. **Catch That Story** - *Tatay Jobo Elizes, publisher* + II. **Obit** - *Bambi Harper, Famous columnist* + III. **Speech, UP, 2003** - *Butch Jimenez, PLDT Executive* + IV. **Speech, Silliman U, 2006** - *Butch Jimenez, PLDT Executive* + V. **The Mission Moment** - *Dr. Phil Stack, Psyhologist* + VI. **Writing Underground** - *Mila D. Aguilar, Poet & Writer* + VII. **Academic Freedom** - *Mila Aguilar, Poet & Writer* + VIII. **Subanon Spirits of Rice & Land** - *Noel Cornel Alegre, Academician* + IX. **I Look Out The Window** - *Atty. Toto Causing, Lawyer, Journalist & Writer* + X. **Ride On A Bus, Poem** - *Anonymous via Melanie Ferrer, Budding Poet* + XI. **Why Am I Doing This** - *Susie Barbieri, Social Activist* + XII. **How To Court A Philipine Lady** - *Rodel Ramos & Jose Torres, Civic Leaders* + XIII. **Inspiring Young Filipino Entrepreneur** - *Lloyd Luna, Motivational Speaker* + XIV. **The Success Story of Ian Del Carmen** - *Lloyd Luna, Motivational Speaker* + XV. **Story of Bacna Surgical Mission** - *Sylvia Salvador, Civic Leader* + XVI. **1987 Philippine Constitution** - *Full Text (Special Feature)* + XVII. **Why Publish Writings** - *Tatay Jobo Elizes, Publisher*

Writings 2 Book, 2009 + I. **Why Can't We Act Up Together** - *Susie Barbieri, Social Activist* + II. **I Know Where They Are All Going** - *Cesar Lumba, Writer & Poet* + III. **There Is Hope For The Philippines** - *Grace Padaca, Isabela Governor* + IV. **Pointers On Employment Abroad** - *Melanie Aquino, Dentist & Writer* + V. **Without KNCHS: (Love story)** - *Atty. Toto Causing, Jury Proponent, Writer* + VI. **422 Years Ago** - *Rodel Rodis, Writer & Political activist* + VII. **Filipino American History Month** - *Rodel Rodis, Writer & Political activist* + VIII. **Love is the Next Truth, poem** - *Daniel Rodis, son of Rodel* + IX. **A Need For Reflection - Gloom** - *Cesar Torres, Politial Activist, academician* + X. **Our Purpose Driven Life** - *Joey Concepcion, RFM Pres. & GoNegosyo activist* + XI. **Did Ninoy Die For Nothing** - *Joey Concepcion, RFM Head & GoNegosyo Activist* + XII. **Why The Filipino Voted** - *Pablito Lim, Zambales Businessman* + XIII. **Life And Love, Poem** - *Nannette Yatco, Dentist, Fine Artist, Poet* + XIV. **Criteria - American Institute of Philanthropy** - *Charity Guidelines (Feature)* + XV. **Strangers In Our Own Country** - *Casiano Mayor Jr., Author & Writer* + XVI. **Coming Revolution In The Ballot** - *Cesar Lumba, Author & Writer* + XVII. **2009 - A Retrospective** - *Cesar Lumba, Author & Writer* + XVIII. **All Over The World** - *Vicente Rivera Jr., Short Story Writer* + XIX. **Harvest** - *Loreto Paras Sulit, Short Story Writer* + XX. **Things Your Burglar Won't Tell** - *Jude Tagaciudad, Writer* + XXI. **The Gypsy Soul** - *Casiano Mayor Jr., Author & Writer* + XXII. **An End To Cheating** - *Sonny Coloma, Academician & Writer* + XXIII. **Toward Culture of Giving** - *Sonny Coloma, Academician & Writer*

Writings 3A Book, 2012 + + 1. **EPIC25, Emerging Philippines Investors Coalition**, *Norman Madrid* + + 2. **Management Ability As An Issue**, *Dr. Rene B. Azurin* + + 3. **Do We Really Want To Give Our Politicos More Power**, *Dr. Rene B. Azurin* + + 4. **Will 2010 Fulfill Filipinos High Hopes For Better Life – Metamorphosis**, *Ernie D. Delfin* + + 5. **Comelec Is The Root Of All Evils**, *Toto Causing* + + 6. **Some Advantages of Federalism and Parliamentary Government For The Philippines**, *Dr. Jose Abueva* + + 7. **Sometimes A Great Nation**, *Mar-Vic Cagurangan* + + 8. **Great Conspiracy**, *Mar-Vic Cagurangan* + + 9. **Of Speech & Life's Riddles**, *Casiano Mayor* + + 10. **Bad Start To The Year**, *Rod Garcia* + + 11. **A Dinner out**, *Rod Garcia* + + 12. **One More Time**, *Roy Gaane* + + 13. **Strange Noises** – *Tatay Jobo Elizes* + +

Writings 3B Book, 2012 + + 1. **The Reeds and Beams of Sunset in Paite and Balangaging in Zambales**, *Ceres Busa* + + 2. **Memories of your Past**, *Ceres Busa* + + 3. **Blowout in the Barrio**, *Ceres Busa* + + 4. **Dream on Sari-sari Store Keeper**, *Ceres Busa* + + 5. **O Naraniag O Bulan**, *Ceres Busa*, + + 6. **Candelaria, O Candelaria**, *Ceres Busa* + 7. **Four P's ... Pastillas, Pilipig, Patupat at Panan**, *Ceres Busa* + + 8. **On Being Filipino American**, *John Reyes* + + 9. **The Monterey Peninsula**, *John Reyes* + + 10. **The Salaza Fiesta**, *John Reyes* + + 11. **Salawikain: Filipino Proverbs**, *John Reyes* + + 12. **Musikero (The Musician)**, *John Reyes* + + 13. **Did You Know (1)**, *Bert Guiang* + + 14. **Did You Know (2)**, *Bert Guiang* + + 15. **Did You Know (3)**, *Bert Guiang* + + 16. **Did You Know (4)**, *Bert Guiang* + + 17. **Did You Know (5)**, *Bert Guiang* + + 18. **Sharing Trivia**, *Bert Guiang* + +

Irineo P. Goce (aka Ka Pule 2 and Leonidas Agbayani) + + + 16, Random Sayings & Advices,

Solo Authored Books: + Book A - **Turning Points - Empty Dreams** - *Job Elizes Sr,1968 (Reissue 2009)* + +Book B - **Be Considerate - Behaviour Issues** - *Tatay Jobo Elizes (Jr), 2009* + +Book C - **Piglets Unlimited - Wealth Untapped** - *Tatay Jobo Elizes, 2009* + + Book D - **Out of the Misty Sea We Must** - *Cesar Lumba. 2010* + +Book E - **Fulfilled** - *Gonzales Reynaldo, Editor, 2010* + + Dook F - **Reflections** - *Bert Guiang, 2010* + + Book G - **Writings 7 - My Vintage Pics** - *Tatay Jobo Elizes, 2010* + + Book H - **May Bagwis Ang Pag-ibig** - *Percival C. Cruz* + + Book I - **Letters To Matrimony** - *Irineo Perez Coce, Ka Pule2, 2011* + + Book J - **Songs I Wish You Knew** - *Soledad R. Juan, 2011* + + Book K - **Make My Day** - *Larry Henares Jr., 1993, Re-issue 2011* + + Book L - **Our Guerrero Family** - *Tatay Jobo Elizes* + + Book M - **Joketor 1** - *Tatay Jobo Elizes, 2011* + + Book N - **Fave Art-1** - *Tatay Jobo Elizes, 2011* + + Book O - **Beyond idle thoughts**, *by MLMunoz, Sept,2011* + + Book P - **Cracks In The Armor**, *Mariano Ngan, Oct 2011* + + **Book Q, Fave Art-2**, *Tatay Jobo Elizes, Nov.2011*

Writings 12 Book, April 2012 + + **1. Twenty Excuses Filipinos Use**, *Orion Perez Dumdum* + + **2. One By One, The Petals Drop**, *Julia C. Lagoc* + + **3. Religion & the Scientist**, *Honorio M. Cruz, MD* + + **4. The Tales of the Aswang & Bangungot**, *Honorio M. Cruz, MD* + + **5. Sex & Politics**, *Honrio M. Cruz, MD* + + **6. Autopsy**, *Ben Gonzales, MD* + + **7. Geekmocracy**, *Mar-Vic Cagurangan* + + **8. Flights: Voice from the Future that Lives in the Past**, *Mar-Vic Cagurangan* + + **9. Kaya Natin! Sanctuary**, *Marisa Lerias* + + **10. The Days of Courage**, *Gerry Partido* + + **11. Earth Day and the Tragedy of a Famous River**, *Cesar D. Candari, MD, FCAP Emeritus* + + **12. Few Filipino-American NonprofitsGetting Political**, *Erwin De Leon* + + **13. Filipino-American Political Invisibility And Community Organizations**, *Erwin De Leon* I+ + **14. I'm 32 and I am still a Virgin**, *Jovelyn Bayubay Revilla* + + **15. Hiding Ill-Gotten Wealth**, *Jobo Elizes*

Writings 13 Book, July 2012 + + **1. From "Criminal" to "Doctor" in Criminal Justice**, *Raymundo E. Narag* + + **2. The Essence of Giving**, *MLMunoz* + + **3. My Prescription for Spiritual Life**, *Sonja Barbara dL Munoz* + + **4. Anak Ng Prosti**, *Pamela Joy Agtoto* + + **5. Ang Kapangyarihan ng Kanyang Pag-ibig**, *Percival Campoamor Cruz* + + **6. Ang Tato ni Apo Pule**, *Percival Campoamor Cruz* + + **7. Rapture**, *Percival Campoamor Cruz* + + **8. Ang Taong Walang Anino**, *Percival Campoamor Cruz* + + **9. Gender Formula – Boy or Girl**, *Tatay Jobo Elizes* + + **10. The Single**, *Jhackie Eslit Bayobay* + + **11. Why I Am Angry**, *Jhackie Eslit Bayobay*, **12. Rules of Living**, *Jhackie Eslit Bayobay* + + **13. Being Alone**, *Jhackie Eslit Bayobay* + + **14. Love and Hurt**, *Jhackie Eslit Bayobay* + + **15. My First Heart Aches**, *Jhackie Eslit Bayobay* + + **16. Why the Philippines Need Sex Education**, *Reygel Saplad Perales* + +

Timely Writings 14, 2013 + + **1. The Giant Sucking Sound and the Rise of Employnomics**, *Cesar Fernando Lumba* + + **2. UP, College of Bus. Admin. and Cesar E.A. Virata**, *Eugenio Pulmano* + + **3. The Missing Element in Education Reform**, *Late Sec. Jesse Robredo* + + **4. China: Some Observations from My Recent Trip**, *Antonio Nievera* + + **5. Don't invest in stocks if you don't have these**, *Alvin T. Tabanag* + + **6. Creating Your Own Financial Plan**, *Alvin T. Tabanag* + + **7. Anti-Gay Hate Crimes on the Rise in New York City: A Call to the Community**, *Kevin L. Nadal, Ph.D.* + + **8. Native Colonialism & Subjugation**, *Anonymous (TJ Friend)* + + **9. The Way We Were - Fond Look at a Hometown**, *Fred Natividad & Bing Castillo* + + **10. Obituary: Common Sense**, *Anonymous* + + **11. Be The Best Ever**, *Anonymous* + + **12. Remembering Capt. Rene N. Jarque**, *Ellen Tordesillas* + + **13. Why I Left the Military**, *Late Capt. Rene N. Jarque* + + **14. Soldiers In Elections: From Pawns to Knights**, *Late Capt. Rene N. Jarque* + + **15. Reforming The Armed Forces** - *Late Capt. Rene N. Jarque* + +

Timeless Writings-15 (TW15), 2014 + + **1. Protecting the Nation's Marine Wealth in the West Philippine Sea**, *SC Justice Antonio T. Carpio* + + **2. Are Filipinos United Against China's Invasion of Ayungin Shoal**, *Rodel Rodis* + + **3. Telltale Signs: Why are there So Many Nurses in the US?**, *Rodel Rodis* + + **4. Telltale Signs: Philippines - A Jewish Refugee from the Holocaust**, *Rodel Rodis* + + **5. Telltale Signs: OFW Remittances Promote Mendicant Culture**, *Rodel Rodis* + + **6. Adding Insult to Injury: UP College Named After Marcos' Prime Minister**, *Ted Laguatan* + + **7. Aguino to Nation: "This is your SONA"**, *Pres. Benigno Aquino III* + + **8. Why We Are Poor A Purpose for the Middle Class**, *F. Sionil Jose* + + **9. Secrets of a Romantic Man**, *Dr. Phil Stack* + + **10. Totoong Buhay sa Canada**, *Racz Kelly* + + **11. Small Steps to Building a Nation**, *Bert Armada* + + **12. The Rising of a Nation**, *Bert Armada*

Solo Authored Books: + + +

Book A, **Turning Points**, *Job Elizes Sr,1968 (Reissue 2009)* + + + Book B, **Be Considerate For Once**, *Tatay Jobo Elizes (Jr), 2013* Book C, **Piglets Unlimited - Wealth**, *Tatay Jobo Elizes, 2009* + + + Book D, **Out of the Misty Sea We Must**, *Cesar Lumba, 2010* + + + Book E, **Fulfilled** – *Gonzales Reynaldo, Editor, 2010* + + + Book F - **Reflections** - *Bert Guiang, 2010* + + + Book G, **Writings 7 - My Vintage Pics**, *Tatay Jobo Elizes, 2010* + Book H, **May Bagwis Ang Pag-ibig**, *Percival C. Cruz* + + + Book I, **Letters To Matrimony**, *Irineo P. Goce, Ka Pule2, 2011* + Book J, **Songs I Wish You Knew**, *Soledad R. Juan, 2011* + + + Book K, **Make My Day**, *Larry Henares Jr., 1993, Re-issue 2011* + Book L, **Our Guerrero Family**, *Tatay Jobo Elizes, 2010* + + Book M, **Handy Jokes**, *Tatay J. Elizes, 2011* + Book N, **FaveArt 1**, *Tatay Jobo Elizes, 2011* + + Book O, **Beyond idle thoughts**, *MLMunoz, Sept,2011* + + + Book P, **Cracks In The Armor**, *Mariano Ngan, Oct 2011* + + Book Q, **FaveArt 2**, *Tatay Jobo Elizes, 2011* + + Book R, **Balitang Kutsero**, *Perry Diaz, Jan 2012* + + + Book S, **FaveArt3**, *Tatay Jobo, 2011* + + + Book T, **FaveArt4** ,*2012, Tatay Jobo* + + + Book U, **Stack Family Journals**, *Phil & Fe Stack, 2012* + + + Book V, **Emily, An Adoption Journey**, *Romerl Elizes, 2012* + + + Book W, **Hermes Alegre Art Gallery**, *TJ & Hermes, 2012* + + + Book X, **Masaya Din, Malungkot Din**, *Jovelyn B. Revilla, 2012* Book Y, **Tiis, Sipag At Tiyaga**, *Raquel Delfin Padilla, 2012* + + + Book Z, **Until I Meet You**, *Jhackie Eslit Bayobay, 2012* + + + Book AA, **Buhay At Pag-ibig**, *Argel Lucero Tamayo, 2012* + + + Book AB, **Hail to the Second Best**, *Dr. Philip Stack, 2012* + + + Book AC, **Life Bus**, *Mommy Joyce Pineda-Faulmino, 2012* + + + Book AD, **My Candid Musings**, *Monette Dioquino Calugay, 2012* + Book AE, **Tickets to Life**, *Maria Lourdes Jesalva, 2012* + + + Book AF, **The Dove Files**, *Mike Portes, 2012* + + + Book AG, **Nursing Vignettes**, *Jocelyn Cerrudo Sese, 2012* + Book AH, **Poor Ba Us**, *R.A. Gubalane, 2012* + + + Book AI, **Summer Idyll**, *Avelina Gil, 2012* + + Book AJ, **Legacy (Pamana)**, *Rachel Astrero, 2012* + + Book AK, **Narratives Old & New**, *Avelina J. Gil, 2013* + + Book AL, **Buhay Saudi**, *Adele J. Esic, 2013* + + Book AM, **Buhay Ofw Atbp**, *Jessica Napat, 2013* + + Book AN, **Mga Tula Ng Buhay**, *Angelita C. Esguerra, 2013* + + Book AO, **Not by Bread Alone**, *Judge Lily V. Magtolis, 2013* + + Book AP, **Jokes Collection-2**, *Tatay Jobo Elizes, 2013* + + + Book AR, *My Writings Sometimes*, *Tatay Jobo Elizes, 2013* + + Book AS, **Sa 'Yo Na Ako**, *Shayne A. Martinez, 2013* + + Book AT, **My Kin's Family Trees**, *Tatay Jobo Elizes, 2013* + + Book AU, **Rizal Family Tree & Others**, *Tatay Jobo Elizes, 2013* + + Book AV, **Make My Day-2, Nice & Nasty**, *L. Henares, 2013 (1993)* + + Book AW, **Make My Day-3, Cecilia, Love**, *L.Henares, 2013 (1993)*Book AX, **Handy Lyrics-1**, *Tatay Jobo Elizes, 2013* + + Book AY, **Ang Biblos**, *Rev. Dr. Eugenio Guerrero, 2014 (1929)* + + Book AZ, **Make My Day-4**, *Sweet & Sour*, *L. Henares, 2014 (1993)* + + Book BA, **Life's Journey, True Stories**, *Dr. Phil Stack, 2014* + + Book BB, **Gerry Gil Writings, 2014**, *Danny Gil* + + Book BC, **Mr. President**, *Hermie Rotea, 2014* + + Book BD, **Nostalgic Pics 1**, *Tatay Jobo Elizes, 2014* + + Book BE, **MakeMyDay-5, Saints & Sinners**, *Henares, 2014 (1993)* + + Book BF, **MakeMyDay-6, Villains & Heroes**, *Henares, 2014 (1993)* + + Book BG, **Nostalgic Pics 2 (ElizesClan)**, *TatayJE, 2014* + + Book BH, **MakeMyDay-7, Tough & Tender**, *Henares, 2014(1993)* + + Book BI, **MakeMyDay-8, Light & Shadow**, *Henares, 2014(1993)* + + Book BJ, **MakeMyDay-9, Give & Take**, *Henares, 2014(1993)* + + Book BK, **MakeMyDay-10, ToBeOrNotToBe**, *Henares, 2014(1993)* + Book BL, **Emily Forever In Love, Poems**,*Emily Espanol Derry, 2013* + + Book BM, **The Sinatra Songbook**, *Henares, 2014* + + Book BN, **The Gaborro Reader**, *Allen Gaborro, 2010*

Publisher: **Tatay Jobo Elizes** was born in Manila, Philippines, in 1934, retiree, now based in NY, busy self-publishing and involved in piglets dispersal programs in Philippines.
Acknowledgement & Dedication: Gratitude and acknowledgment belongs to those who support my hobby publishing books and charities. I heartily dedicate this to my wife, **Cora**, my children, **Tetchie, Chevy & Abeth, and Marie & Bimbo**, my grandchildren, **Karines & Aung, Noelle, Chad, Marjo, Jeb, Marvin & Marty**, great-grandsons **Jason Win & Carson** and my siblings **Susan, Hilda, Bobby, Bey & Manny** and to all my extended relatives.
ISBN Code. Printed in the United States of America under ISBN code below. Copies of paintings are available in the public domain.
ISBN-13: 978-1468128277 + + + ISBN-10: 1468128272
Self-Publisher's List - Contact job_elizes@yahoo.com, tatay@usa.com
My websites: http://tinyurl.com/mj76ccq + + + www.jobelizes.com

www.ingramcontent.com/pod-product-compliance
Lightning Source LLC
Chambersburg PA
CBHW051108180526
45172CB00002B/827